C000062155

CONTENTS

STAINED GLASS

Roger Rosewell

SHIRE PUBLICATIONS

Published by Shire Publications Ltd,
PO Box 883, Oxford, OX1 9PL, UK
PO Box 3985, New York, NY 10185-3985, USA
Email: shire@shirebooks.co.uk   www.shirebooks.co.uk

First published 2012.
2nd impression 2013.
Transferred to digital print on demand 2015.

A CIP catalogue record for this book is available from the
British Library.

Shire Library no. 686.   ISBN-13: 978 0 74781 147 3

Roger Rosewell has asserted his right under the
Copyright, Designs and Patents Act, 1988, to be identified
as the author of this book.

Designed by Tony Truscott Designs, Sussex, UK.
Typeset in Perpetua and Gill Sans.
Printed and bound by PrintOnDemand-Worldwide.com,
Peterborough, UK.

COVER IMAGE
Henry of Fordwich arrives at the shrine, c. 1213–20,
Canterbury Cathedral, Kent.

TITLE PAGE IMAGE
Detail from the Last Judgement by Clayton & Bell, 1860,
St Mary, Hanley Castle, Worcestershire.

DEDICATION
To Christine Anne Huddleston.

ACKNOWLEDGEMENTS
Thanks to Peter Cormack, Painton Cowen, Anna Eavis,
Robin Fleet, Geoffrey Lane, C.B. Newham, Adrian Rose,
Harriet Rosewell, Joseph Spooner, Lyn Stilgoe, and Aidan
McRae Thomson.

I am grateful to the vicars, priests and churchwardens
whose windows appear in this book. Photographs also
appear by permission of the Dean and Chapter of the
Cathedrals of Birmingham (St Philip), Canterbury,
Coventry, Ely, Gloucester, Lincoln, Manchester, Oxford,
Wells and York Minster; the Warden and Fellows of All
Souls College, Merton College and New College at
Oxford, and the Warden and Fellows of Winchester
College; the Provost and Scholars of King's College
Cambridge; the Vicar and Churchwardens of Tewkesbury
Abbey; the Churches Conservation Trust; and the Trustees
of the Stained Glass Museum at Ely Cathedral.

All images are © the author.

Shire Publications is supporting the Woodland Trust, the UK's leading woodland conservation charity, by funding the dedication of trees.

INTRODUCTION

FOR OVER A THOUSAND YEARS painted and stained glass has filled the windows of English cathedrals and churches with sacred stories and vivid images of great moments in national history.

These masterpieces of colour and design were produced by artists who painted with light to create monuments that have inspired generations of audiences.

They include the largest collection of surviving medieval paintings in England and some of greatest masterpieces of modern art.

Whether small and delicate or towering and powerful, these windows transform buildings and change the way we see and feel.

Apart from their religious significance, stained glass windows also provide a dramatic record of the people whose beliefs and passions shaped England for a millennium. They are unique lights into our past.

5

ANGLO-SAXON WINDOW GLASS, AD 700–1066

TRYING TO PIECE TOGETHER the early history of stained glass is like looking through a misted window on a rainy day. Not everything is clear; much cannot be seen. A twelfth-century manuscript says that window glass was installed at York Minster as early as AD 669–72 to prevent 'the entry of birds and showers', but for most historians the story begins a few decades later, during the construction of a new monastery at the mouth of the river Wear, now part of modern Sunderland. According to a near-contemporary account of these events written by the Venerable Bede, a monk at the adjacent 'twin' monastery of Jarrow:

> When the work [at Wearmouth] was drawing to completion, he [Abbot Benedict] sent messengers to Gaul [probably Normandy] to fetch glaziers, craftsmen who were at this time unknown in Britain, that they might glaze the windows of his church, choir and refectory. This was done and they came, and they not only finished the work required, but from this caused the English to know and learn their handicraft ....

Over two thousand pieces of white and coloured window glass have been recovered by archaeologists from the Wearmouth and Jarrow sites. The colours include blue of several hues, green, amber, yellow-brown and red. Scientific analysis has shown that it was made from recycled broken glass, possibly salvaged from abandoned fifth-century Roman buildings, and chunks of raw glass imported from the eastern Mediterranean (modern-day Egypt, Jordan and Israel), the main centre of commercial glass production before the ninth century.

How this raw glass got to Northumbria remains a fascinating mystery. It is thought to have been exported from the Middle East to northern France before crossing the Channel and edging its way along the eastern coast of England by ship.

Once the glass had been unloaded, it was processed and cut into small shapes – square, rectangular, triangular, diamond, and curved – known as *quarries*. It seems likely that the separate pieces were then arranged into a decorative 'mosaic' pattern, with the individual quarries held together by a framework of lead strips. Formed in H-shaped sections, these lead supports are known as 'cames' (from the Latin *calamus*, meaning 'reed'), and the lines they formed around the cut pieces of glass were often used as integral parts of the overall design.

At the Anglo-Saxon church of St Paul at Jarrow, some of the excavated fragments have been assembled in this manner and installed in a small circular window. It is a conjectural scheme, rather than a replica of any original design, and is the oldest window glass in England.

Apart from these finds, Anglo-Saxon window glass dating from the seventh to eleventh centuries has been recovered from sixteen other sites across England. A fragment excavated at Winchester, dated by archaeologists to *c*. AD 966–1066, is painted with acanthus leaf foliage of the same type as appears in Anglo-Saxon manuscripts of the same period.

The origin of this later glass is unclear, as glass making had begun to spread to northern Europe about this time. Although there is virtually no evidence for the manufacture of glass in England in Anglo-Saxon times, the production of clear (white) glass was widespread in the Wealden forests of Surrey and Kent from the thirteenth to seventeenth centuries, and in Staffordshire from the early fourteenth century to the seventeenth century.

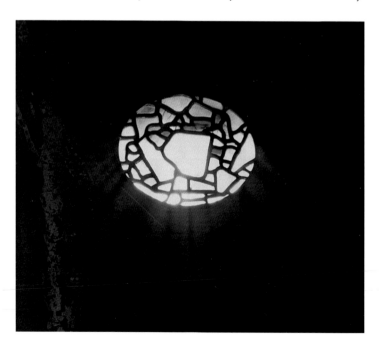

Anglo-Saxon glass, *c*. AD 700, St Paul, Jarrow, Tyne and Wear.

THE NORMANS, 1066–1200

IN CONTRAST TO FRANCE, very little Norman painted glass survives in England from the hundred years after the Conquest in 1066. There is a small figure of the Archangel St Michael at Dalbury (Derbyshire) dated to c. 1100–35, and four windows in Canterbury Cathedral, possibly made around 1150–60. These are the earliest complete stained glass windows in England.

Both sets of windows incorporate 'pot-metal' coloured glass, the description given to glass that was coloured during the production process by the addition of various metal oxides to the clay melting pot: iron oxide made red; copper oxide green or yellow; cobalt (aluminium oxide) produced blue; and magnesium purple. For reasons not entirely clear, these processes were never developed in medieval England and every piece of coloured glass used in church windows had to be imported, often from the Rouen area in Normandy, but also from Burgundy, Hesse and Lorraine. From the end of the fifteenth century Venetian glass was available in London.

Sadly the evidence for the next fifty years is again extremely scarce; it was a time of profound innovation in the architecture of churches and the display of stained glass. At the time of the Conquest, an art and architectural style based on Roman models, known as 'Romanesque', dominated Europe (in England it is often called 'Norman'), in which walls were massive and window openings relatively small with rounded arches.

All changed when the great abbey church of Saint-Denis, near Paris, was rebuilt in the 1140s, and emerging new architectural ideas coalesced. The use of pointed arches and flying buttresses meant that walls could be opened up for tall lancet windows. For many Christian writers, such as an unknown twelfth-century German poet at Arnstein Abbey, streams of light passing through glass became a metaphor for Christ's Immaculate Conception and his birth to a Virgin mother.

Whoever thinks this is impossible
shall only have a look on the glass, which is similar to you:
the sun beams are shining through the glass

it is intact as it was before
through the intact glass it [the light] falls into the house
the darkness it banishes from there ...
You are the intact glass, where the light came from
to take away darkness from the world.

Church intellectuals and glaziers eagerly devised new schemes to fill the spaces created by these larger windows. Although most of the original glazing has been lost, late-twelfth-century glass at York Minster and Canterbury Cathedral, together with early-thirteenth-century glass at Lincoln Cathedral and Beverley Minster (Yorkshire), provide important insights into the artistic styles, designs and techniques prevalent at this time.

The subjects depicted in these windows were chosen by highly sophisticated theologians. They were designed to enhance and define sacred spaces with glowing colours and stories, to honour patron saints, to encase worshippers in holiness, and to remind monks and priests of scriptural doctrines and Christian devotion.

YORK MINSTER, 1180–90

At York Minster one of the most important schemes showed an image of the human ancestry of Christ known as the Tree of Jesse, with the recumbent figure of the Old Testament figure of Jesse, the father of David, lying at the foot of the window while a tree winds its way upwards from him depicting figures of kings and prophets before reaching the figures of the Virgin Mary and Christ at the summit. Visual depictions of Christ's human ancestry springing 'from the stem of Jesse' were often associated with the transmission of 'wisdom', devotion to the Virgin Mary and evidence of Christ's appearance in human flesh.

Other themes at the Minster were typical of what appeared elsewhere in greater churches on both sides of the Channel: scenes from the Old Testament; events from the Infancy and Passion (suffering) of Christ; and the Last Judgement, the moment when the dead would be summoned from their graves to learn their fate – eternal bliss with God, or everlasting damnation in the terrors and stench of hell. Remains of scenes depicting episodes from the lives of three saints, St Martin, St Nicholas and St Benedict, also survive. Images of saints were a mainstay of most medieval window schemes. Saints were cherished as guardians, protectors, and intercessors between humans and God. Their relics, such as bones, were believed to have miracle-working powers. A compendium of their lives compiled in the 1260s, the *Legenda Aurea* (Golden Legend), became the international bestseller of the Middle Ages, helping to influence both the choice and the iconography of images.

Panel showing
a king, from the
Tree of Jesse
(face repainted),
c. 1180–90, York
Minster Museum.

CANTERBURY CATHEDRAL, 1170–1220

Outstanding examples of late twelfth- and early thirteenth-century glass survive at Canterbury Cathedral, much of it dating to a fifty-year period after a fire in 1174 gutted the church. As the walls were rebuilt, new windows were installed in the choir (sometimes spelled 'quire', the western part of the chancel between the nave and the high altar), both transepts and several chapels at the eastern end of the church. The similarity between some of the figures in the uppermost clerestory windows of the new choir, and others in the choir of the Abbey of Saint-Remi at Reims, 80 miles east of Paris, suggests that the glass painters were either French or had been deeply influenced by projects in north-east France.

The glass painters would have begun by making sketches of the scheme, known by the sixteenth century as a *vidimus* (literally 'we have seen'). Once the designs had been approved, full-size cartoons or templates for the glass were drawn out on whitewashed boards or trestle tables. The cartoon would show where the different pieces of coloured or plain glass would fit and where the cut lead lines should be made. Great care was taken to ensure that

11

these lines enhanced the design rather than detracting from it. The glass was cut by drawing a hot iron across the surface and then snapping or breaking it into shape. Rough edges were trimmed by a hook-shaped metal tool known as a 'grozing iron', which leaves a characteristic 'bitten' edge. (Diamond cutters were unknown in northern Europe until they were imported from Italy c. 1500.)

Once the glass had been cut and the pieces arranged, an artist would paint the details of faces, drapery folds, and background patterns, usually on the interior face of the glass. The paint was either black or brown. Washes of thinner paint were often smeared over the glass to hold or diffuse light and to prevent unwanted glare. Until the introduction of silver (yellow) stain in the early fourteenth century and the use of coloured enamel paints in the sixteenth century (see pages 25 and 26), no other colours were employed.

A number of manuals or treatises on glass painting survive from the twelfth century onwards, which describe these techniques. The earliest is by a German monk, Theophilus, whose *De Diversis Artibus* ('On various arts') explained how glass paint should be made from copper oxide and ground glass mixed with wine (probably vinegar) or urine. A sixteenth-century Flemish recipe for the manufacture of this same type of paint shows that little had changed in the intervening half millennium. It stipulated one part of iron oxide powder collected from a blacksmith's anvil and half a part of high-lead glass powder, mixed together and ground again with '*schlechten Wasser*' ('bad water', urine perhaps) for three hours before a tiny amount of gum arabic was dissolved into the mixture. The paint was ready to use after the mixture had been left to stand a night and a day in a covered dish. Once the paint had been applied, it was fused to the glass in a hot kiln.

Theophilus also described how to make lettering by covering an area of glass with a wash of paint and then using the handle of the paintbrush or a pointed stick ('stickwork') to scratch names and other captions. Similar techniques were used to draw patterns.

The first major scheme at Canterbury was a sequence of Christ's ancestors on earth in the clerestory of the choir. Forty-three of the original eighty-six figures survive. The series began with Adam, where the lead lines have been incorporated into the design to delineate his rib cage and his name inscribed in the way outlined above. The posture of some of the other figures in the cycle is more akin to sculpture. The scheme stressed the incarnation of Christ as God's son on earth and the hope of redemption and salvation.

Elsewhere in the cathedral a complex set of twelve biblical 'typological' windows, made before 1180, paired scenes from the Old Testament ('types') with scenes from the New Testament ('anti-types') to show how events in the former foretold or prefigured events in the latter. The rigorous study of typology was very popular in educated circles between the twelfth and sixteenth centuries; scholars pored over the Old Testament to find parallels with the later New Testament accounts of Christ's Infancy, Ministry and Passion. A good example includes the pairing of Moses leading the Israelites from slavery out of Egypt and towards the Promised Land, with Christ leading the Gentiles (non-Jews) from their pagan gods towards the true Church.

Some of the scenes in these windows were painted by the artist who painted Adam; others have been attributed to an artist whose elongated figures with small heads can be seen in the Parable of the Sower window, in which seeds represent the Word of God (those falling on stony ground are eaten by birds, while those falling on rich soil bear fruit for those who understand it). The window is also significant for its attempts to portray receding landscapes.

Adam delving, c. 1175–80, Canterbury Cathedral, Kent.

Many of the panels shimmer with the skill of these remarkable painters. The depiction of flames in the window depicting the Old Testament story of God's destruction of the wicked cities of Sodom and Gomorrah is typical. Glass makers and painters needed considerable time and skill to create this effect. First, the flames had to be cut from imported pot-metal red or ruby glass, which, unlike other colours, had been added,

Christer leading the
Gentiles, c. 1175–
80, Canterbury
Cathedral, Kent.

Strips of different-
coloured glass set
diagonally to
create the effect
of a receding
landscape, Parable
of the Sower,
c. 1175–80,
Canterbury
Cathedral, Kent.

or 'flashed', to a piece of white glass during the manufacturing process to achieve translucency. Next, the painter had to grind, scratch, or 'abrade' areas of the red layer until the white glass was revealed below and the impression of a blazing inferno created.

Other schemes painted in the cathedral around this time include two circular windows in the north and south transepts, the *oculi* or eyes – so called because, unlike a circular rose window, they do not include any stone tracery. The north window showed scenes of the Old Law represented by Moses and the female figure of *Synagogia*, symbolising the Jewish church, while the south *oculus* celebrated the triumph of the New Law represented by Christ and the Christian church (*Ecclesia*).

A final scheme made between between 1184 and summer 1220 had a different purpose. After years of clashes between the two men over the rights and privileges of the Church, on 29 December 1170 Thomas Becket, the Archbishop of Canterbury, was brutally murdered in the cathedral by knights loyal to Henry II. The killing shocked Christian Europe. In 1172 a penitent Henry was ritually flogged by the monks and a year later the Pope canonised Becket as a saint and declared him to be 'a martyr for the church'.

At the same time miraculous cures were attributed to Becket's blood and pilgrims began flocking to Canterbury. In 1220 the saint's body was moved from a tomb in the crypt to a lustrous gold shrine in the newly built Trinity Chapel behind the high altar at the eastern end of the church.

The destruction of Sodom and Gomorrah, c. 1175–80, Canterbury Cathedral, Kent.

As an added refinement the chapel was enclosed by twelve lancet windows depicting scenes from St Thomas's life and martyrdom and the miracles attributed to him. The scenes were held in place by metal frames known as armatures which were arranged to create different designs, including circles and canted squares. The result was a rich, dim light of luminous colours which intensified the sense of awe for people visiting the shrine. The miracle scenes were based on records compiled by the monks and included cures for toothache, lameness, epilepsy, madness and blindness. Seven original windows survive. They show the saint's marble shrine with 'crawl holes' along its side, into which the sick and suffering could insert the limb they hoped would be cured.

Among the miracle windows is the story of the cure of Henry of Fordwich, a town near Canterbury. One panel (see cover) shows 'Mad Henry' being dragged towards the shrine. The drama of the scene is summarised in the inscription running along the top of the architectural screen: *amens accedit* ('he arrives out of his mind'). The adjoining scene illustrates the curative effects of a night spent before the shrine. Here, Henry is shown in calm prayer as one of his 'friends' and the supervising monk look at each other in stunned disbelief at the transformation that has taken place. Again, the meaning of the scene is identified by an inscription near the top of the panel reading '*Orat, sanus(que) recedit*' ('He prays, and departs sane').

Such stories helped Canterbury become one of the most visited – and wealthiest – pilgrim sites in Europe. Other churches with miracle-working shrines installed similar schemes. A window of c. 1414 at York Minster shows pilgrims seeking cures at the shrine of St William, a twelfth-century archbishop of the diocese – see page 34.

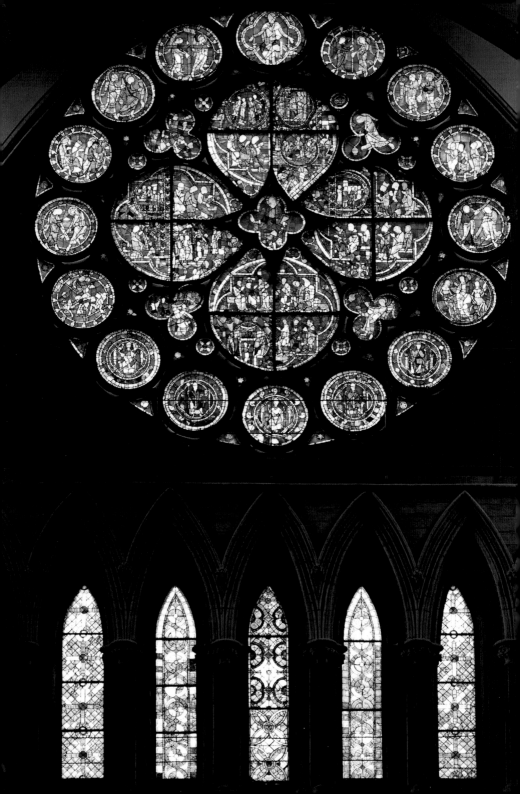

THE EARLY THIRTEENTH CENTURY

WHILE MANY IN THE CHURCH revelled in the opulence of coloured glass, the followers of St Bernard of Clairvaux (1090–1153), a charismatic French abbot, repudiated any kind of lavish display in their monasteries. Under statutes adopted *c.* 1145–51 they stipulated that only unpainted white grisaille glass (from the French *gris*, 'grey') should be allowed in Cistercian churches such as Fountains Abbey in Yorkshire. Plain glass was seen as symbolising the truth and purity of God, and less likely to distract monks from their prayers, although ornamental patterns formed from latticing and interlacing straps made entirely by the lead lines were permitted. At Kirkby-in-Furness (Cumbria, formerly Lancashire), a parish church with Cistercian affiliations, a mid- to late twelfth-century Latin cross depicted solely in lead lines is possibly the oldest decorative glass remaining from any window in the whole of the north-west of England.

Again, although not a Cistercian monastery, when Salisbury Cathedral (Wiltshire) was built between 1220 and 1258 its choir aisles and nave windows were filled with grisaille glass. The designers wanted a glazing scheme which would produce a sparkling silvery light conducive to prayer and contemplation.

Although often used as a cheaper alternative to full-coloured glass, the complexity of cutting, painting and leading-up some of the sophisticated geometric grisaille patterns at Salisbury demanded considerable skill. At least sixteen of these designs survive and many are extremely intricate, with decorative layers superimposed and overlapping one another. Some designs consist entirely of lead cut-lines for the patterns: other designs are painted. By contrast, coloured figural glass in the cathedral seems to have been reserved for windows above altars where relics were kept. A panel dated *c.* 1220–36 depicting the stoning of St Stephen, the first Christian martyr, which was probably made for a chapel dedicated to him at the eastern end of the south aisle, was saved after its removal in the 1780s and can now be seen in the parish church of St Leonard at Grateley (Hampshire).

Opposite:
North transept
rose window,
c. 1220–35,
Lincoln Cathedral.

Right: Geometric grisaille window, c. 1200–50, original location unknown, the Stained Glass Museum, Ely Cathedral, Cambridgeshire.

Below: Grisaille panels, c. 1225–58, Salisbury Cathedral, Wiltshire.

Below right: The martyrdom of St Stephen, c. 1220–36, St Leonard, Grateley, Hampshire.

Another spectacular grisaille scheme of the mid-thirteenth century survives in five lancet windows ('the Five Sisters') in the north transept of York Minster. The panels include stylised leaf designs within inventive geometric frameworks formed by strips of coloured glass.

Other surviving glass from this period can be seen at Lincoln Cathedral, which includes a thirteenth-century rose window originally depicting the Last Judgement, and Beverley Minster (Yorkshire), where some panels in the east window show scenes from the legends of St Martin and St Nicholas.

By contrast to the ornate schemes in cathedrals and wealthy abbeys, less is known about the glazing of parish churches in the early thirteenth century. Although small amounts of glass from 1170 to 1250 can be found in many parts of the country, it seems that most openings were enclosed by wooden shutters. When glass was installed, grisaille schemes

predominated. Full-coloured windows were rare and those that have survived are less sophisticated than those in cathedrals and abbeys. Subjects which can be seen in parish churches include scenes from the lives of Christ and the Virgin Mary, with good examples surviving at Ashbourne (Derbyshire) and Aldermaston (Berkshire). Madley (Herefordshire) has scenes from the life of St John and a chancel window at Saxlingham Nethergate (Norfolk) has panels depicting the martyrdom of St Edmund, a ninth-century Christian king of East Anglia, who was said to have been shot to death with arrows by Viking invaders until he 'resembled a porcupine'.

St Edmund with the arrows of his martyrdom, c. 1250, St Mary, Saxlingham Nethergate, Norfolk.

The 'Five Sisters' window, c. 1250, York Minster.

19

THE DECORATED STYLE, 1250–1380

THE GLAZING of the rebuilt Westminster Abbey in the 1250s by Henry III marks a milestone in the history of stained glass in England. Although very little original glass survives, the project was extremely well documented by royal clerks. For the first time we know the names of some of the glass painters, how much they were paid and the cost of the glass itself. For example, from February to July 1253, between thirteen and fifteen glaziers were employed weekly. In August a smaller number were paid at a piecework rate of 8d per square foot for working with coloured glass and 4d for white glass.

As importantly, the scheme also featured shields depicting the royal arms, making it one of the first recorded instances of heraldry in stained glass, a feature which soon began to be a standard component of many medieval (and later) window designs. The insertion of his arms in the windows asserted the king's generosity as the donor of the glass (and building) and reminded worshippers to remember him in their prayers. Other members of the ruling elite followed his lead, sometimes including the royal arms as declarations of their loyalty to the crown. Good displays of heraldic glass can be seen at Dorchester Abbey in Oxfordshire (1300–20) and at Bristol Cathedral (c. 1360).

Finally, the Westminster Abbey architects incorporated French-style bar tracery windows into the church, making much larger spaces available for glazing than before. Typical designs consisted of tall, narrow lancet windows separated by vertical mullions forging a decorative mesh at the head of the window, chiefly consisting of circles or leaf-like lobes such as trefoils.

The following century saw a huge number of sumptuous glazing schemes installed in major cathedrals and monasteries such as Exeter, Wells, Tewkesbury and Gloucester, where significant amounts of glass survive. More parish churches were fitted with painted glass; the arms of the donors often appear in the west window. The overall design, figure style and ornamental features of these windows is known as the Decorated style.

Opposite:
Robert Fitzhamon,
c. 1340–4,
Tewkesbury Abbey,
Gloucestershire.

The royal arms,
c. 1270–80,
St Mary and
St Nicholas,
Chetwode,
Buckinghamshire.

When the chapter house of Salisbury Cathedral was glazed in the late 1260s, figures of past bishops and kings appeared in the tracery lights, and the larger windows were filled with coloured heraldic arms surrounded by grisaille patterns. The scheme recalled the cathedral's history and thanked the donors who had funded its construction.

Towards the end of the century an innovative scheme of 'band

Band windows,
c. 1300–10, Merton
College Chapel,
Oxford.

windows', combining coloured and grisaille glass, was introduced in the chapter house at York Minster. Pioneered in France around 1265, it consisted of horizontal bands of rectangular panels of narrative coloured glass sandwiched between layers of grisaille glass, making interiors lighter while at the same time retaining the windows as a setting for storytelling.

This effect can also be seen in another largely complete band window scheme of *c.* 1300–10 in the chapel at Merton College, Oxford, where another French invention was deployed: the display of individual figures under elaborate canopies. Inspired by developments in sculpture and metalwork, this refinement sought to integrate window imagery with other architectural and decorative features such as carved and painted woodwork and stonework.

Donor figure
under canopy,
c. 1300–10, Merton
College Chapel,
Oxford.

Initially such canopies were simple but eventually they grew into spectacular confections until by the fifteenth century they included carved bases and capitals, elaborate side shafts, traceried windows, battlements, flying buttresses, turrets and pinnacles, even tiny figures.

The glazing of the nave at York Minster was undertaken between 1305 and 1330. Band windows proliferated. Some designs resemble those painted in contemporary manuscript

Canopy with carved head in the capital, c. 1330, All Saints, Icklingham, Suffolk.

Canopy with niche figures of peasants, c. 1340–9, Lady Chapel, Ely Cathedral, Cambridgeshire.

illuminations. One border shows a monkey inspecting a uroscopy flask, aping medieval physicians who purported to diagnose ailments by analysing the smell, colour and opacity of urine. The designer of the scheme married satire with sermonising, reminding audiences that only Christ could heal men of their sins and they should look through or beyond the glass to the spiritual salvation that the church provided.

Monkey inspecting a uroscopy flask, c. 1310–20, York Minster.

Other important glass of this date includes the glazing of the chancel at Norbury (Derbyshire) in *c.* 1300 and the installation of the new east window at Exeter Cathedral in 1304.

At Norbury the local lord of the manor, Sir Henry Fitzherbert (d. *c.* 1315), commissioned eight windows showing twenty-six shields set within grisaille glass. The people remembered were Sir Henry's commanders and comrades from the wars against Scotland in 1291–1301 and possibly other campaigns in Wales and Gascony. They were intended to demonstrate fealty, kinship and social networks, and to secure intercession for the fallen.

The Exeter glazing is the best pre-Reformation painted glass in Devon. According to records kept in the cathedral, just over 3,950 feet of glass from Rouen was bought between 1301 and 1304 for use in the eastern part of the church. In 1304, the master glazier, Walter, was paid £4 10s 'For setting the glass of the high gable [the Great East Window], eight high windows [the choir clerestory] and six windows of the aisles of the new work [the windows of the north and south ambulatory behind the high altar]'. Although the east window had to be replaced less than a hundred years later because of masonry decay, nine figures from the original scheme were reused and still survive.

New approaches to colour also appeared in the first decades of the fourteenth century, with the rich reds, blues and purples of earlier schemes replaced by earthy tones of red-brown to soft purple (known as 'murrey'), yellow and leafy green, and the emergence of a new colouring technique which transformed glazing schemes for ever.

This breakthrough was imported from France after Parisian-based artists had applied a traditional eastern Mediterranean recipe for staining vessel glass to colouring window glass. By painting different amounts of silver or silver oxide compounds on the external face of white glass they discovered that stains ranging from pale lemon to rich orange could be produced after firing. The possibilities it opened up were endless. Instead of glaziers laboriously cutting separate pieces of yellow glass to depict hair or crowns, the application of silver oxide on the back of a head painted on white glass could easily create golden hair, a saintly halo or a pronged crown. A window with an inscription date of 1313 at the parish church at Le Mesnil-Villeman, in Normandy, is the earliest documented example of this technique in Europe. Without similar evidence, it is impossible to say

when the technique was introduced into England but certainly by the 1320s it was gathering momentum. The chancel glazing of the parish church at Stanford-on-Avon (Northamptonshire), one of the best preserved schemes of this date, includes silver stain in the borders and in some of the foliage in the grisaille. Later glaziers applied the stain to blue glass to produce shades of green. Together with abrading, this technique proved invaluable for creating accurately tinted heraldic windows. Other benefits included opportunities

Opposite page: St John the Baptist, c. 1475, Browne's Hospital, Stamford, Lincolnshire. Note the silver stain decoration of the halo, hem of cloak, cross and book, and the side shafts of the canopy with lions and eagles.

Left: Heraldic and grisaille glass, c. 1300, St Mary and St Barlock, Norbury, Derbyshire.

Left: The crucified Christ from the Tree of Jesse, c. 1320–40, Wells Cathedral, Somerset.

27

to create luxuriously decorated clothing and armour.

Among the great schemes commissioned in the first half of the fourteenth century, the glazing of the eastern arm of Wells Cathedral (Somerset) between the 1320s and 1340s remains remarkably intact. Light and colour were used in a graded way to honour the sacred nature of its settings and as part of the 'language' of the windows. Thus, full colour seems to have been reserved for the east-facing windows, with band windows employed in the side glazing. A powerful example of how colour was used to convey meaning is the Tree of Jesse scheme in the choir of the church. Here the green of the trunk of the tree and the green of the Crucifixion cross link

Above: St Michael weighing souls, c. 1330–5, St Michael and All Angels, Eaton Bishop, Herefordshire.

Right: Band window with saints, grisaille and heraldry, c. 1305, St Mary the Virgin, Selling, Kent.

the images and suggest a third: the Tree of Life. Like glazing schemes before and afterwards, the same cartoons were reused for some of the figural designs.

Another well-preserved scheme was installed at Tewkesbury Abbey, c. 1340–4. Consisting of seven windows in the choir, it includes the Last Judgement in the east window with Old Testament kings, prophets and apostles in the four most immediate side windows witnessing the event. The two remaining windows depict eight lords of Tewkesbury, beginning with the founder of the abbey, Robert Fitzhamon (d. 1107), and including the notorious Hugh Despencer the Younger, who was executed in 1326 by the enemies of Edward II. Each of the eight figures wears an heraldic surcoat and has his hand on a sword. The cartoons were drawn from the same basic model with slight variations. Although such warlike figures may seem out of place in an abbey, the monks celebrated the lords as benefactors of the church, deserving of prayers and emulation, rather than as warrior knights.

Exceptionally fine glazing schemes can also be seen in many parish churches. These include Selling (Kent) and Eaton Bishop (Herefordshire).

The remains of a vigorously painted Tree of Jesse window at Merevale (Warwickshire), dated to 1320–40, is particularly striking, both for its border design of creatures devouring their own bodies and its probable origins in a now demolished Cistercian church that once stood nearby. Erosion of the Order's rigid rules prohibiting coloured glass had begun in the late thirteenth century when heraldry appeared in the windows of some abbeys; by the mid-fourteenth century it had effectively been abandoned after pressure from wealthy patrons who wanted decorative interiors in the churches they endowed.

Border designs, c. 1320–40, Church of Our Lady, Merevale, Warwickshire.

Insect quarries as background. Robert Skelton, Chamberlain of York, donating a window, c. 1350, St Denys, Walmgate, York.

Many of these schemes were painted by well-established professional workshops whose output can be traced across swathes of England. The workshop which made the Merevale glass was also responsible for work in Worcestershire and at Christ Church Cathedral in Oxford, while the artists who worked at Tewkesbury also painted the glass at Eaton Bishop and Moccas, both in Herefordshire. In the north-west of England the output of an otherwise unknown Chester-based workshop has been found at nine sites in the county, including Grappenhall, and another in Flintshire in North Wales.

A guild of master glass painters, which regulated apprenticeships, prices and quality, was known in London by 1328 and centres such as York, Norwich, Oxford and Exeter also seem to have had well-established workshops which supplied churches within their regions and sometimes further afield.

Several other innovations which had lasting effects emerged in the first half of the fourteenth century. The first was the replacement of background grisaille schemes (which had been painted with naturalistic foliage designs such as maple, oak and ivy leaves since about 1280) with small, diamond-shaped white glass quarries painted and silver-stained with more varied motifs such as rosettes, birds and insects (see page 29).

The second was the first documented example of a window inscription in English, rather than Latin, the formal language of the Church. Formerly visible

St Peter, the Virgin and Christ, east window, c. 1350–60, Gloucester Cathedral.

in the east window of Elsing church in Norfolk, it named Sir Hugh Hastings (d. 1347) as the donor of the window. Hastings had fought under Edward III against the French at the battle of Crécy in 1346 and his still-extant brass monument includes images of his comrades-in-arms as mourners, some of whom would later help to found the Order of the Garter, the highest military order in medieval England.

The third quarter of the fourteenth century seems to have been a bleak period in the history of English glass painting, probably caused by the crippling effects of the Black Death in 1348 and recurrent outbursts of the plague in 1361, 1362 and 1369. Artists and patrons were almost certainly among the casualties as more than a third of the population died. It is highly likely that Edward III's recruitment of glass painters from twenty-seven counties to glaze St Stephen's Chapel in the royal complex at Westminster in 1351 was partly due to shortages of master craftsmen in the capital.

The glazing of the east window of Gloucester Abbey (now Cathedral) during that decade may have been influenced by these events. For while the window was filled with familiar images of bishops, monks, saints and apostles, with the arms of prominent nobles at its foot, the scheme was created almost entirely from painted and stained white glass, with the more expensive red and blue pot-metal colours used only for the background

St Katherine, c. 1325, St Mary, Deerhurst, Gloucestershire.

settings. One possibility is that the design sought to harness the translucency of band windows without the bands; another is that economic and political factors, such as the ongoing wars with France, may have forced the glass painters to improvise and adapt. The result remains stunning, a dazzling curtain of glass that soars over the church's high altar, with the tiers of figures in the central section rising higher than the wings, replicating the design of contemporary three-panel altarpieces, known as triptychs.

Here, as elsewhere, English glass painters and designers continued to paint swaying S-type figures copied from French art. Another elegant example can be seen at Deerhurst (Gloucestershire).

However, towards the end of the fourteenth century developments in manuscript illumination culminated in the adoption of a new 'International' style of painting, which spread to England from central Europe in the 1380s.

THE INTERNATIONAL STYLE AND THE RENAISSANCE

THE INTERNATIONAL STYLE (1380–1500)

Nowhere is the adoption of this emerging style better illustrated than in two commissions undertaken towards the end of the century by the same glass painter, Thomas of Oxford, for the same patron, William of Wykeham (1324–84), the Bishop of Winchester. The faces in the first project at Wykeham's New College at Oxford, painted in the 1380s, are markedly different from those Thomas painted at Wykeham's Winchester College in the 1390s. Instead of the linear painting style prevalent in Oxford, the moulding of the Winchester faces was softer and more realistic.

The new style soon appeared in other parts of the country when the Coventry-based glass painter John Thornton introduced it to the north of England and to the Midlands.

Probably recommended by a former Bishop of Coventry who had been promoted to the archbishopric of York, Thornton was hired in 1405 to paint a huge window for the rebuilt eastern end of York Minster. It was a mammoth undertaking, consisting of 144 panels containing approximately 1,680 square feet of glass – in area the size of a tennis court, and probably the largest single expanse of medieval glass ever commissioned in England. Even without the responsibilities of painting and installing such a window within three years, the sheer effort of ordering the glass from the Continent and transporting it to York would have been a major logistical operation.

The window was conceived as a *tour de force* of intellectual Christian knowledge based on St John the Divine's Book of Revelation, which traces the history of the world from the first prophecy to the last: God's final judgement of humankind and the creation of a 'new heaven and earth'. The window was arranged in groups of three, a sacred number symbolising the Holy Trinity: God the Father, God the Son and God the Holy Ghost. Thus three panels of lay and ecclesiastical figures from the history of York shown in three lights made nine, which when multiplied by three produced twenty-seven scenes from the Old Testament, which, multiplied by three, formed eighty-one panels of Apocalypse scenes. The grand total of these was 19,683,

Opposite:
St John the Evangelist, c. 1380–6, New College Chapel, Oxford.

which, by some medieval calculations, equalled the number of years between the Creation and the end of the world.

Apart from the great east window, Thornton and his workshop painted, or influenced, a number of other schemes. His distinctive facial style of small mouths and elongated noses with a bulbous tip can be seen in the ninety-five-panel St William window in York Minster, made around 1414, and in churches scattered across the West and East Midlands, such as Bledington (Oxfordshire) and Thurcaston (Leicestershire).

The glazing of these parish churches was often commissioned by members of the new wealthy middle class, who funded rebuilding campaigns and installed windows which shone with popular religiosity and who frequently appeared as kneeling man-and-wife couples with their hands clasped in prayer alongside the inscription *Orate pro animabus*, asking those who saw the window to pray for their souls. The main aim of such gifts was to reduce the time

The Virgin and Child, *c.* 1393, Winchester College Chapel, Winchester, Hampshire.

Pilgrims seeking cures at St William's shrine, St William window, 1414, York Minster.

the donors spent in purgatory, a sort of anteroom to the Kingdom of God where the dead were purified of their sins before entry.

A unique example of such a window can be seen at All Saints Church, North Street, York, donated by members of two local families whose images appear at the foot of the scheme. Known as the Pricke of Conscience window, it shows the fifteen signs that medieval theologians thought would precede the end of the world. They include fish roaring and the earth catching fire. The window included inscriptions written in English summarising each scene. The texts were based on a poem of the same name written by an anonymous author in the mid-fourteenth century. Although funded by devout lay people, the scheme was probably suggested and overseen by the parish priest.

Detail of a rector, John Mersden (d. 1425), All Saints, Thurcaston, Leicestershire.

Political symbolism in windows also became particularly significant after Richard II (1367–1400) was overthrown in 1399 by his pugnacious cousin, Henry Bolingbroke (*c.* 1366–1413), Duke of Lancaster, crowned as Henry IV.

The new dynasty soon ran into opposition, triggering years of factional resentments which eventually erupted into a vicious civil war – the Wars of the Roses – between supporters of the Lancastrian usurpers and their opponents arrayed behind the Dukes of York, who claimed to be the legitimate heirs to the throne.

The fourth sign, 'Fish make a roaring noise', Pricke of Conscience window, *c.* 1410–20, All Saints, North Street, York.

35

When Henry Chichele (*c*.1362–1443), the Archbishop of Canterbury and an ally of the Lancastrian cause, built All Souls College in Oxford between 1438 and 1442, he included selective images of English kings from Alfred the Great and his grandson, Athelstan, to Henry IV, Henry V and Henry VI in some of the windows, implying that the Lancastrian dynasty was the true heir to these ancient monarchs. Similar propaganda was installed by Lancastrian supporters in the merchant guildhall of St Mary in Coventry, after it had been adopted as the headquarters for the mayor and city leaders.

A different display of Lancastrian allegiance can be seen in the magnificent funerary chapel of Richard Beauchamp, the Earl of Warwick (1382–1439), at the collegiate church of St Mary in the town at the centre of his great estate. Although probably best known for an orchestra of musical angels in the side-window tracery lights, the choice of saints in the east window of the chapel included those with a special appeal to the ruling Lancastrian aristocracy, and to Beauchamp personally, who had supported Henry IV's overthrow of Richard II and fought with his son, Henry V, in France. The figures depicted St Thomas Becket, whose holy oil had sanctified

English kings, including Henry V (centre), c. 1451–61, St Mary's Hall, Coventry, West Midlands.

St Thomas Becket,
c. 1447–64,
St Mary, Warwick.

Right: Jewelling in
the garments of
the Virgin Mary,
c. 1447–64,
St Mary, Warwick.

Below: Detail
of Edward IV,
c. 1482–7,
Canterbury
Cathedral, Kent.

the coronation of Henry IV, and alongside whose shrine in Canterbury the king was buried; St Alban, a favourite of Henry V's brother, Humphrey, Duke of Gloucester; St Winifred, who was credited with curing the future Henry V of a head wound he sustained as a sixteen-year-old at the battle of Shrewsbury (1403); and St John of Bridlington, whose help had been invoked during the battle of Agincourt (1415).

The Beauchamp Chapel glass is stunning for other reasons, particularly the unmatched amounts of 'jewelling' used by the glaziers to enrich the clothing and prestige of the figures. A tricky and time-consuming technique, this process involved drilling and enlarging small holes in a piece of glass, probably with a combination of tools such as a bow-drill and files, before inserting pieces of different coloured glass and then leading them into position – without fracturing the original.

The Warwick scheme was executed by John Prudde, probably the outstanding artist working in stained glass in the middle of the fifteenth century. First documented in the Westminster Abbey accounts in 1426–7, he had been appointed to the post of 'King's Glazier' in 1440 and was paid 12d per day, plus the gift of a gown at Christmas and the occupancy of the glazing shed in Westminster Palace.

Political symbolism changed again after the Yorkist victories in the civil war. Edward IV and his family were shown in windows at Canterbury Cathedral, and men such as the Suffolk clothier, John Clopton (1423–97), who had narrowly avoided execution after being accused of treasonable correspondence with the Lancastrians in 1461, proclaimed their loyalty to the new regime by including the Yorkist badge of the white rose in a sunburst in their stained glass windows.

A poignant reminder of the savagery of these struggles is a window in the former priory church at Little Malvern in Worcestershire, which shows the ill-fated Edward V (1470–83), who, along with his brother, disappeared in the Tower of London (the 'Princes in the Tower') after his uncle had been crowned Richard III. It was painted *c.* 1482–3 by the locally based workshop of Richard Twygge and Thomas Wodshawe. The work of these artists can also be seen at Buckland (Gloucestershire), Great Malvern Priory (Worcestershire), and Tattershall (Lincolnshire) (see pages 42, 45 and 47).

For much of the fifteenth century English artists persisted with insular versions of the International style and often produced windows consisting largely or entirely of delicately painted and silver-stained white glass, for example John Glaysier, probably Thomas of

Left: John Clopton with Yorkist badges, *c.* 1485, Holy Trinity, Long Melford, Suffolk.

Below left: Edward V, 1482–3, St Mary and St Michael, Little Malvern, Worcestershire.

Below: St Anne teaching the Virgin to read, *c.* 1441, the chapel of All Souls College, Oxford.

Oxford's son, who painted the windows of All Souls College Chapel in Oxford in 1441–2.

THE RENAISSANCE (1500–40)

Towards the end of the fifteenth century, the influence of Burgundian and Flemish artists, as well as new Italian Renaissance styles, began to be felt. The most important features were the use of receding perspective techniques, particularly with landscapes, and a painterly approach to subject scenes which treated windows as a single canvas rather than as separate lights. Expressive portrait-like images also appeared.

As demand grew for this type of glazing, Flemish artists settled in England, provoking a fierce reaction from established painters who resented the competition they posed. The London guild went so far as to have some of

Above: The Prophet Amos, c. 1500–15, St Mary, Fairford, Gloucestershire.

Right: Receding perspectives: detail from the Life of St Nicholas, c. 1510–19, All Saints, Hillesden, Buckinghamshire.

the immigrants arrested but in the main the newcomers evaded capture by living on the south side of the Thames at Southwark, beyond the jurisdiction of the City of London and its angry glass painters.

Excellent examples of Anglo-Netherlandish work in English churches can be seen at Fairford (Gloucestershire), the most complete pre-Reformation glazing scheme in a parish church in England; Hillesden (Buckinghamshire); the chapel of The Vyne, a National Trust owned house near Basingstoke (Hampshire); and in the finest scheme made before the advent of the Reformation, the windows of King's College Chapel, Cambridge.

Painted between 1515 and 1546 by Flemish artists, including Galyon Hone (d. 1551/2), who had succeeded Bernard Flower as the King's Glazier in 1517, its completion was a high point in the history of stained glass, both as a refined art and as an established feature of abbeys and cathedrals, parish churches and rural chapels across Britain.

But how such windows were 'seen' by worshippers varied, depending on their visibility and function.

Statue of Henry VI (1515) and north aisle windows, c. 1540, King's College Chapel, Cambridge.

SEEING STAINED GLASS

EYEWITNESS ACCOUNTS of how ordinary medieval people responded to images in stained glass are rare. A letter written by a German nun in the sixteenth century says that when she saw images of the Passion of Christ in the cloister windows of her monastery they helped her to picture the scene in her mind, to walk alongside Him mentally as He carried the cross to Calvary and to thank God for sacrificing His only son to redeem humankind of its sins and offer eternal salvation.

Schemes were often designed according to visibility. Upper-level clerestory windows usually contained either clear white glass or single large figures, as at Canterbury Cathedral, while lower-level windows were filled with pictorial stories or holy images which could be studied at closer quarters.

Some windows were intended to be seen by different audiences. In abbeys, the choir and cloisters were reserved exclusively for monks and nuns; even in parish churches the eastern end, the chancel, was the preserve of the priests, and was separated from the nave by a screen. Many churches also contained private family chapels where access was restricted.

By contrast the Becket windows at Canterbury were intended to be seen by tens of thousands of pilgrims. It is possible that some monks acted as guides, explaining the stories to visitors. Windows in the naves of churches were also intended to be viewed by entire congregations.

The visibility of the windows and their intended audience affected their function. Narrative imagery and stories were often linked to the altars and relics below them. Windows studded with the colours of precious stones caressed these treasures in an opulent light, almost as if they were caskets for the sacred objects.

East windows filled with Crucifixion imagery complemented the sacred rites of the Mass. Priests faced the image of Christ raised on the cross as they raised the consecrated host above their heads. Designs such as the shield of the five wounds also reminded audiences of Christ's suffering and fanned devotional intensity. Some schemes complemented processions and other special ceremonies.

Opposite:
The sacrament of marriage, c. 1485, St Michael, Buckland, Gloucestershire.

Above: Shield of the five wounds, late fifteenth or early sixteenth century, St James, Gawsworth, Cheshire.

Right: Christ crucified on the lily, late fifteenth century, St Mary, Westwood, Wiltshire.

Images of saints sustained worshippers and helped to focus their prayers. Many saints were depicted with their attribute, a symbol which helped to identify them. Thus St Katherine was shown holding a spiked wheel (see page 31), St John the Baptist holding the Lamb of God (see page 26), and St Helena holding a wooden cross, alluding to her discovery during a pilgrimage to the Holy Land of the 'true cross' on which Christ was crucified.

People who gazed upon the Virgin Mary tenderly caring for the Christ child hoped that she would intercede for them in the same way – merciful, gentle, and loving. Some windows featured stories and miracles of her life drawn from accounts such as those in the *Legenda Aurea*. Many showed her being crowned Queen of Heaven (for example the coronation of the Virgin, shown on page 50). At Great Malvern Priory (Worcestershire), a window in the north transept visualised the text of the *Magnificat*, a hymn from the Gospel of St Luke telling the story of the Annunciation.

Some windows stressed the protective role of saints. Images of St George reassured audiences that their country and its soldiers were protected by a holy warrior knight, while images of St Christopher (Greek: Christ-bearer) were thought to have talismanic powers, conferring protection against death before the administration of the Last Rites (Holy Unction) to anyone who saw them.

Other popular saints included the Twelve Apostles, who were shown each holding the article of faith attributed to them from the Apostles' Creed, and images of the Four Doctors of the Church, the title bestowed on Saints Ambrose, Augustine, Gregory and Jerome, in recognition of their scholarly writings.

Windows also expounded the teachings of the Church, such as the seven works of mercy (see later) and its seven sacraments, or sacred rituals – baptism, confirmation, marriage, penance, extreme unction (the last rites before death), eucharist, and ordination. Examples of these survive at Buckland (Gloucestershire), Cartmel Fell (Cumbria), Crudwell (Wiltshire), Doddiscombsleigh (Devon) and Melbury Bubb (Dorset).

Subjects more usually found in wall paintings, such as the warning to gossips or janglers, which admonished worshippers not to chatter in church (Stanford-on-Avon, Northamptonshire),

St Christopher carrying the Christ child across a swirling river, c. 1467–77, St Peter, Stockerston, Leicestershire.

Detail of the *Magnificat* window, 1501–2, Great Malvern Priory, Worcestershire.

45

Devils and chattering women, in a warning to janglers, c. 1330–50, St Nicholas, Stanford-on-Avon, Northamptonshire.

and the warning to sabbath breakers, entreating Christians not to work or gamble on the Sabbath lest they add to Christ's wounds, also appeared (St Neot, Cornwall, currently on loan to the Royal Cornwall Museum in Truro).

In a few instances window glass contained the texts of prayers which, if repeated, earned the viewer an 'indulgence', a reduction in the time they would otherwise spend in purgatory. A now-lost inscription in a window at the church of St Cuthbert at Fishlake, South Yorkshire, promised a thirty-day pardon to all those who added 'Jesu' to their 'Ave Maria' prayer. Although there are instances of people giving money for candles to be lit in front of images in windows, usually a sign of prayer, figures in stained glass were not usually seen as objects of devotion, in the same way as life-like statues.

Context, location and timings were critical. As mentioned earlier, congregations were separated from the chancel and high altar of the church by a screen surmounted by a cross known as the Rood showing the crucified Christ hanging on the cross, flanked by his mother, the Virgin Mary, and St John the Evangelist. At York Minster worshippers would have seen the great east window with its message of Judgement and the promise of a new world through this image of the Crucifixion, inexorably linking the events together.

Although stained glass windows are often said to be stories in pictures for people who could not read, the reality was more complex. Images could have layers of meaning, making it unclear what different audiences might have 'read' in them. Growing literacy rates and the rise of a devout and educated middle class must also be considered. The twelfth-century typological windows at Canterbury included Latin inscriptions and were intended for a small, scholarly audience well-versed in biblical studies. Four hundred years later the inclusion of typological scenes at Tattershall and Fairford implies that the audience for such ideas was much greater, particularly among lay people who owned books.

Whether people could read was often beside the point. For most people stories were not learned from images, but orally. Once recognised and understood, the window imagery would help audiences to remember such stories and cement their meaning and significance. Such windows, together with others showing the Apostles' Creed, were visual mnemonic aids when worshippers were quizzed by their parish priest about the core beliefs of their faith.

This included schemes showing the seven works of mercy (feed the hungry, give drink to the thirsty, clothe the naked, visit prisoners, care for the sick, house the homeless, and bury the dead), which extolled Christian virtues, as at All Saints, North Street, York, and at Combs (Suffolk), and Tattershall (Lincolnshire). Those depicting the seven deadly sins (pride, envy, anger, lust, avarice, sloth, and gluttony), as at Newark-on-Trent (Nottinghamshire) (see page 5), or the horrors of hell, as at Fairford (Gloucestershire), counselled what not to do and why!

Other windows were intended to be seen in two ways: for the holiness of the images they depicted, and for the benefits they brought for the

Feeding the hungry, from the seven works of mercy, c. 1480–2, Holy Trinity, Tattershall, Lincolnshire.

47

donors who had given the glass in the expectation that they would be remembered in the prayers of viewers. A late-fifteenth-century donor image at Waterperry (Oxfordshire) highlights the care that could be taken with such paintings. Although it was probably not intended to be an actual

Hell mouth,
c. 1500–15,
St Mary, Fairford,
Gloucestershire.

portrait, Margaret FitzEllis is shown wearing a fashionable 'butterfly' headdress which encloses her temples in a stiff cloth (buckram) overlaid by a veil of fine linen gauze. The artist has painted the buckram pattern on both the inner and outer faces of the glass (backpainting) to create an impression of three-dimensional depth. In addition, a matt black wash has been spread over the yellow stained glass in her headband so that a pattern could be traced through the paint using a pointed stick ('stickwork').

Detail of Margaret FitzEllis, c. 1470, St Mary, Waterperry, Oxfordshire.

Sometimes groups, or confraternities, of people donated windows. Examples include the Palmers' (or Pilgrims') Guild windows at Ludlow (Shropshire) and a series of windows at St Neot (Cornwall) given in the 1520s by the young men, their sisters and wives who lived in the western part of the parish.

In some instances glass could be 'signed' with a rebus, a visual pun on the donor's name. Good examples of the latter are several fifteenth-century windows at Weston-on-Avon (Warwickshire), crammed with repetitive images of a cook's table mounted on a ship, signifying that they were the gifts of the local Cooksey family. Initials or merchants' marks also appeared, for example at St Thomas, Salisbury (Wiltshire) and Stanford-on-Avon (Northamptonshire).

The inclusion of heraldry and donor images in windows might also emphasise the genealogy of a family, especially if shown in conjunction with images of Christ's earthly family (the Holy Kindred) as at Thornhill (Yorkshire). In abbeys and cathedrals, heraldic windows recorded the identity of donors and promised prayers for those who gave money or land to the church.

Cooksey rebus, fifteenth century, All Saints, Weston-on-Avon, Warwickshire.

Irrespective of anything else, painted windows beautified churches, set them apart from other buildings, helped to inspire a sense of divine mystery and intensified the presence of the miraculous. They illuminated darkness and sanctified light, induced devotion and reminded viewers of Christian stories and beliefs. They brought reassurance and hope. Such glass had been accumulated and maintained for centuries and was one of the greatest artistic achievements of medieval England.

STAINED GLASS AND OTHER ARTS

THE RELATIONSHIP between painted glass and complementary arts such as architecture, wall paintings and sculpture was nuanced. Although they sometimes formed a completely integrated design, on most occasions the artistic decoration of churches evolved over long periods with different patrons and artists adding their own imprints.

As a general rule, glass painters planned their schemes to fit window spaces designed by architects, not the other way around, although it seems likely that many window openings were deliberately conceived as cages or stage sets for extravagant displays of painted glass. An exception to this presumption can be seen at Wing (Buckinghamshire), where the design of a

The Coronation of the Virgin, with the arms of the Warenne family (Earls of Surrey), c. 1320, All Saints, Wing, Buckinghamshire.

window dating from the early fourteenth century seems to have been enlarged specifically to accommodate the arms of the patrons of the church.

Changes in architectural styles created opportunities for new designs. The emergence of Perpendicular architecture in the mid-fourteenth century saw the creation of large windows with extensive tracery lights. Designers filled these lights with decorative patterns, heraldry and images of saints and angels. The latter frequently appeared playing musical instruments, singing hymns, or holding armorial shields. Sometimes a complete scheme depicting the nine orders of angels was installed. Based on sixth-century writings, this concept divided angels into different groups, with each hierarchy having a specific responsibility: seraphim; cherubim; thrones; dominations (or dominions); virtues; powers (*potestates*); principalities; archangels; angels.

While wall paintings were often conceived and executed separately from stained glass, some schemes complemented one another. At York Minster the chapter house included both wall paintings and stained glass windows acknowledging powerful benefactors to the church. At Hailes (Gloucestershire) paintings of angels swinging incense burners in the splays of the east window may have been adoring a now-lost sacred image in the adjacent glass.

Above left: Angel musician with a psaltery (type of zither), c. 1460–70, St Agnes, Cawston, Norfolk.

Above: Armoured angel from the *potestates* (powers) hierarchy thrashing a devil, c. 1441–50, St Peter and St Paul, Salle, Norfolk.

51

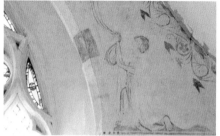

Many schemes were devised in conjunction with monuments and sculpture. Examples of sculptural effigies or memorial brasses commissioned at the same time as commemorative stained glass are relatively

Wall painting of an angel swinging an incense burner, fourteenth century, Hailes, Gloucestershire.

The Tree of Jesse window, c. 1320–40, Dorchester Abbey, Oxfordshire.

common, as at Warwick. An unusual example of integrated sculpture and stained glass can be seen at Dorchester Abbey (Oxfordshire). A Tree of Jesse window of 1320–40 consists of stonework carved to resemble a tree, with Jesse at the bottom, twenty carved figures in the upright mullions, and space for a further twenty-two painted figures in the glass lights, totalling the forty-two generations of Christ's earthly ancestors mentioned in the gospel of St Matthew, Chapter 1.

Some designs for stained glass were inspired by artists working in different media such as manuscript illumination – occasionally the traffic was two-way, especially in the eleventh and twelfth centuries. A number of the images in a 105-panel window in York Minster made in the 1440s depicting the Life of St Cuthbert appear to be copies of illustrations in a twelfth-century manuscript of the same title made for Durham Cathedral Priory. A woodblock book dating from *c.* 1460 and often, if misleadingly, called the *Biblia Pauperum* ('Poor Man's Bible'), as it was neither a Bible nor intended for poor people, included a series of typological images that were reproduced by stained-glass artists at Fairford (Gloucestershire) and Tattershall (Lincolnshire). A window from the latter church, now at St Martin, Stamford (Lincolnshire), shows the Old Testament story of Samson escaping from the city of Gaza, corresponding with Christ's escape from His tomb during the Miracle of the Resurrection.

Woodblock illustration of Samson carrying the gates of Gaza, from the *Biblia Pauperum*, *c.* 1460. This image is thought to have inspired several windows, including the one below.

Samson carrying the gates of Gaza, *c.* 1466–80, St Martin, Stamford, Lincolnshire.

REFORMATION, RENEWAL AND DESTRUCTION, 1538–1660

I N 1534 Henry VIII (1491–1547) renounced the Pope in Rome and proclaimed himself 'Supreme Head of the English Church'. Within a few years, thousands of windows had been destroyed by a combination of politics, greed and the fervent Protestant religious beliefs (the Reformation) which convulsed northern Europe in the 1530s.

The first wave of destruction began in 1538 when Henry condemned Becket as a traitor and ordered the obliteration of his shrine at Canterbury. As part of the same purge churches were ordered to erase the archbishop's name and 'put down' all his images, whether in glass, wood or in words. Among the windows lost were a set chronicling the saint's life and martyrdom, including a scene of Henry II's flogging, at the hospital church of St Thomas of Acon in London, built over the site of Becket's birth. The 1552–3 churchwarden accounts for St John's Ber Street, Norwich, include a payment of 19s for 'making of a glass window wherein Thomas Becket was'. Fortunately a handful of windows remained unscathed, including a scene of the saint's murder at Checkley (Staffordshire).

The martyrdom of St Thomas Becket, c. 1320, St Mary and All Saints, Checkley, Staffordshire.

The dissolution of the monasteries (1536–40) unleashed another crackle of destruction when abbeys such as Bury St Edmunds in Suffolk and the cathedral priory church in Coventry were demolished. Contemporary accounts record the fate of the glass after the monks had left. At Rievaulx Abbey (Yorkshire), it was 'layd up under lok and key and kept out of danger' before being categorised as to be kept, sold or melted down for lead. At Thorney Abbey (Cambridgeshire) a furnace was set up on site to extract silver from the lead cames. 'Xxviii panys of payntyd glasses' were among the contents valued and removed from Merevale Abbey (Warwickshire) by agents working for the king.

Some glass was saved, however, when abbey churches were converted to parish churches, as at Tewkesbury and Great Malvern, or if panels were bought and installed in nearby churches, as at Morley (Derbyshire), and Merevale (Warwickshire).

Greater losses were to follow. Although the Reformation of the Church had begun during Henry's reign, attacks on traditional Catholic beliefs concerning purgatory and the miraculous powers of saints intensified after the accession of his nine-year-old son, Edward VI, in 1547. Now the edicts were unequivocal: churches were instructed to 'take away, utterly extinct and destroy all shrines ... pictures, paintings and all other monuments of feigned miracles, pilgrimages, idolatry or superstition so that there remain no memory of the same in walls, glass windows ...'. In 1552–3 the church wardens of St Michael at Plea in Norwich spent £20 replacing seventeen windows 'wherein were contained the lives of certain profane histories'.

Although large numbers of windows were shattered in the wake of these injunctions, the scale of the attack varied. In some areas offensive images were whitewashed out rather than removed, as at Mileham (Norfolk). Elsewhere only the heads of figures were broken. Sometimes window glass was dismantled and hidden for safe-keeping.

However, despite a complete reversal of Edward's policies after the accession of his Catholic half-sister, Mary I, very few new windows seem to have been made to replace those lost. When Elizabeth I succeeded her in 1558 the previous Protestant policies were reinstated, albeit less extremely. Windows which had survived were allowed to remain because of the cost of replacing them, and new glass was either plain or heraldic.

Half a century of upheaval and confusion, allied to changing tastes and new techniques, had profound consequences for stained glass artists and their art. The first was a dramatic shrinkage of work after 1540. Some painters embraced the new mood, like James Nicholson, who had worked at King's College and became a printer of Protestant books. Others, such as Galyon Hone, saw their incomes plummet as commissions shrivelled. By the time of Elizabeth's death in 1603, the craft had dwindled to a core of glass painters in London and York, fulfilling mainly heraldic commissions and working in quite a different way from their medieval predecessors.

The greatest change was the type of paint they used. Whereas medieval artists had worked in either black or brown pigments and relied upon pot-metal glass and silver staining for colours, Elizabethan glaziers used translucent enamel paints, consisting of ground glass and coloured pigments, which allowed them to paint colours directly onto glass as if they were painting on wood or canvas. The enamels were then fired onto the glass. Typical schemes consisted of white glass painted with enamels and silver stain for the detailed work and large sheets of coloured pot-metal glass for the background settings.

Detail from 'Jonah before Nineveh', by Abraham van Linge, 1630s, Christ Church, Oxford.

Heraldic commissions were uncontroversial, but when religious figural glass reappeared in London in 1613–14 it lit a slow-burning fuse for a rerun of the bitter clashes of the sixteenth century.

Among the new commissions which appeared were a number of schemes painted by the artists Bernard van Linge and his kinsman, Abraham van Linge, originally from Emden in Germany. The east window at Wadham College, Oxford, commissioned in 1621, is signed by Bernard while others in the city at Lincoln College and Christ Church are by Abraham. Both men used a combination of pot-metal glass (for large areas of drapery) and enamel colours painted directly onto rectangular panes of clear glass, so reducing the design role of leads.

English glass painters active around this time include Richard Butler (d. 1638), who made windows for the chapel of Lincoln's Inn (London), and Richard Greenbury (d. 1670), who made a set of saints for the antechapel windows at Magdalen College, Oxford. Six panels painted in 1621 for the chapel of Lord Maynard's stately home at Easton Lodge and attributed to Baptist Sutton (d. 1667) were installed in the local parish church of Little Easton (Essex) in 1857. Other windows by Sutton are in the Abbot's Hospital, Guildford (Surrey), and possibly at Apethorpe (Northamptonshire).

The revival of 'beauty in holiness' was encouraged by Archbishop William Laud (1573–1645), but after being accused of idolatry he was arrested by his Puritan critics in 1641 and churches were ordered to remove 'scandalous pictures', including recently painted windows. An anonymous broadsheet pleaded:

Come honest Glazier, we must crave your aid,
To help us pull these popish windows down.

The Civil Wars which tore England apart in the mid-1640s saw huge amounts of glass destroyed. Cathedrals such as Worcester, Lichfield and Peterborough suffered catastrophic vandalism.

In East Anglia a parliamentary commissioner, William Dowsing (1596–1668), visited over two hundred churches in 1643 and 1644 smashing glass and statues which had survived Reformation iconoclasts. At Sudbury his journal recorded a typical entry: 'We brake down 19 mighty great angels in glass, in all, 80.'

Sir Robert Harley (1579–1656), the Chairman of the Committee for the Demolition of Monuments of Superstition and Idolatry in London, seems to have been particularly ferocious. At his country estate in Leintwardine, Herefordshire, the glass was taken out of the church, 'broken small with a hammer' and then thrown into the River Teme. In the capital itself he is said to have jumped up and down on a piece of painted glass from St Margaret's church, Westminster, treading it to pieces and crowing that he was 'dancing a jig to Laud'.

Another notable iconoclast was Richard Culmer (1597–1662), who boasted of battering windows in Canterbury Cathedral. Fortunately there, as in York Minster, the damage was minimal. Despite being a Royalist stronghold, most of York's historic fabric was preserved after the city's surrender in July 1644 to the parliamentary commander, Lord Fairfax, a Yorkshireman who loved the city and its treasures. Led by the Minster, York now houses the best collection of medieval stained glass in England.

Frustra pilate manus; cor mundum vult Deus

Frustra Pilate manus; cor mundum vult Deus (In vain does Pilate wash his hands; God wants a pure heart), probably by Baptist Sutton, 1621, St Mary, Little Easton, Essex.

Elsewhere glass was hidden to save it from the iconoclasts. At University College, Oxford, a set of windows by Abraham van Linge of 1641 was secreted in a store-room until the 1660s, when they resurfaced, apparently undamaged. At East Harling in Norfolk important fifteenth-century windows were saved from Dowsing's squad of 'breakers' by a local family who hid them in their home.

Sadly the same cannot be said of Scotland and Ireland, where the destruction was particularly thorough. Not a single piece of medieval glass now survives *in situ* in Ireland and the situation in Scotland is barely any better.

Among the many consequences of these losses is that what we see today is but a small percentage of what once existed. Huge numbers of magnificent schemes in cathedrals, abbeys and parish churches have disappeared without trace or record.

INTERREGNUM, 1660–1800

THE HUNDRED YEARS which followed the restoration of the monarchy in 1660 were by past standards uneventful.

Although designers of new churches, such as Sir Christopher Wren (1632–1723), preferred plain glass windows – his masterpiece, St Paul's Cathedral, rebuilt after the Great Fire of London in 1666, had no stained glass whatsoever – heraldic windows continued to be commissioned. An impressive example was made in 1664 by the London glass painter John Oliver (1616/17–1701) at Northill (Bedfordshire), where the arms of the Grocers' Company were installed in the east window, before being moved to the nave in 1880. Henry Gyles (1645–1709), a York-based artist, produced heraldic schemes and a number of attractive painted sundials. A displaced sundial (lacking its central gnomon) by an unknown artist, dating from the 1660s, can be seen at Merton (Norfolk). The scheme includes a fly and a spider with the inscription *Dum loquimur fugit hora* (while we talk, time flies). Much later, in 1795, a heraldic scheme of etched glass by the Birmingham-based glass painter Francis Eginton (1737–1805) was installed by the Earl of Radnor at Great Coxwell (Oxfordshire).

All too often, however, when lead supports weakened and windows needed repair, plumbers and glaziers replaced older painted glass with plain glass, cheaper and easier to install and more in keeping with the prevailing aesthetic taste. Neglect and indifference also took a heavy toll. The spectacular fifteenth-century east window of Great Malvern Priory (Worcestershire) was shattered after a tree was allowed to grow through some missing panels. When the architect James Wyatt (1746–1813) restored Salisbury Cathedral in the 1790s, cartloads of medieval glass were dumped in the town ditch.

Despite such indifference, a contemporary of Gyles, William Price the Elder (d. 1722), described as one of only four glass painters in London in 1683, kept the art alive. Six scenes from his life of Christ painted in 1702 can be seen in the antechapel of Merton College, Oxford, and there are coats of arms by him in Middle Temple Hall (City of London), signed and dated 1698,

Opposite:
The Assumption
of the Virgin by
Francis Eginton,
1795, St Alkmund,
Shrewsbury,
Shropshire.

59

and the hall of Trinity College, Cambridge (1703). Other members of the family included his son Joshua (d. 1722), who painted ten enamel windows after oil sketches by the Italian artist Francesco Sleter (1685–1775), now in the parish church of St Michael at Great Witley (Worcestershire), and his

Arms of the Grocers' Company, by John Oliver, 1664, St Mary the Virgin, Northill, Bedfordshire. Originally the east window, it was set in an iron frame in the south aisle in 1880.

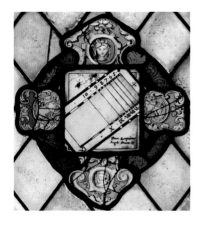

Far left: Sundial, artist unknown, 1660s, St Peter, Merton, Norfolk.

Left: Etched heraldry, by Francis Eginton, 1795, St Giles, Great Coxwell, Oxfordshire.

grandson, William Price (the younger) (?1703–65), who painted the great west window of Westminster Abbey (1735–6). Another important artist was the York-based glass painter William Peckitt (1731–96), who was responsible for a window depicting the Last Supper (1771) in the chapel of Audley End House (Essex), after a design by Biagio Rebecca (1734/5–1808), a member of the Royal Academy.

A distinctive feature of these windows was that they increasingly resembled oil paintings on glass. The east window of St Alkmund,

St Peter healing a cripple, window signed 'J Price 1719', St Michael, Great Witley, Worcestershire.

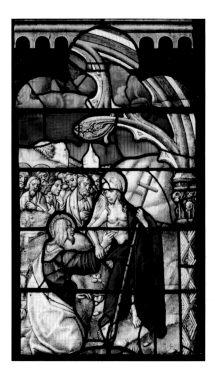

Above: Doubting Thomas, formerly at Steinfeld Abbey, now at St Andrew, Hingham, Norfolk.

Above right: St Bernard rids Foigny of a plague of flies, formerly at Altenburg Abbey, now at St Mary, Shrewsbury, Shropshire.

Shrewsbury, painted in 1795 by Francis Eginton, is a copy of the Assumption of the Virgin by the Italian painter Guido Reni (1575–1642). Similarly, the west window of New College Chapel, Oxford, was painted by Thomas Jervais (d. 1799) in 1783, to designs for the 'Nativity' and the 'Virtues' by Sir Joshua Reynolds (1723–92).

At Lichfield Cathedral, the style was taken to its extreme conclusion when a now-lost window painted in 1795 by Eginton was treated as if it were an oil painting and framed by curtains, prompting critics to quip that the Lady Chapel resembled a drawing room.

A quite separate development surfaced in the second quarter of the eighteenth century: the collection and display of old stained glass by antiquarians such as Horace Walpole (1717–97), the son of Britain's first official Prime Minister, who filled the windows of his home at Strawberry Hill on the western outskirts of London with a medley of different pieces, both English and foreign. Like many subsequent collectors, Walpole liked old glass for its history and decorative effects rather than its religious appeal and displayed it accordingly.

The French Revolution of 1789 and the wars it spawned across Europe fed this growing market for ancient stained glass. When Napoleon's armies invaded what is now Belgium and the western edges of Germany (the Rhineland) they systematically closed monasteries and confiscated church property. In the chaos that followed, large amounts of displaced stained glass poured on to the international art market, much of it finding its way to England. Some enterprising Norfolk businessmen, John Christopher Hampp (1750–1825) and William Stevenson (c. 1750–1821), scavenged the Continent buying glass by the crate-load and selling it to wealthy collectors. One such buyer was Lord Brownlow, who installed displaced sixteenth-century German Renaissance glass in the chapel at his home at Ashridge Park, Hertfordshire. In 1928 this entire collection was bought by the philanthropist Ernest Cook (1865–1955), the grandson of Thomas Cook of travel agency fame, and given to the Victoria and Albert Museum in London. Other consignments found their way into a number of Norfolk churches, such as Hingham and Kimberley, and eventually, by different routes, to St Mary (Shrewsbury), and Stoke d'Abernon (Surrey).

Perhaps the most sensational story involved Lichfield Cathedral. When the Peace of Amiens in 1802 brought a temporary truce to fighting between England and Napoleonic France, the sixteenth-century Renaissance glass from Herkenrode Abbey, near Liège in Belgium, was bought by Sir Brooke Boothby, an English aristocrat who had fled abroad to avoid his creditors, and sold to the cathedral for the bargain price of £200.

Good imported French glass can be seen at Rivenhall (Essex), Twycross (Leicestershire), and Wilton (Wiltshire). The last-named includes displaced twelfth-century panels from the Abbey of Saint-Denis in Paris.

Thousands of sixteenth-century Netherlandish roundels, single panels of clear glass, typically 10 inches in diameter, painted by Dutch and Flemish artists working in centres such as Antwerp and Brussels, were also acquired. Many of the designs were inspired by drawings or engravings created by famous Flemish artists such as Jan Gossaert (d. 1532) and Dirick Vellert (d. 1547). They included both religious and mythological subjects. Early examples often combined extremely delicate glass-painting with an extensive use of silver stain, but by the seventeenth and eighteenth centuries fashions had changed and the use of coloured enamel paints had become widespread. Good collections can be seen at Addington (Buckinghamshire), Rownhams (Hampshire), Nowton (Suffolk) and Malpas (Cheshire).

The beheading of John the Baptist, after Jan Gossaert, c. 1520, St Oswald, Malpas, Cheshire.

RECOVERY AND MASS PRODUCTION, 1800-1900

G LASS PAINTING in the 1780s and early years of the nineteenth century continued to be dominated by artists using enamel colours and recreating either heraldry or oil paintings on glass, but rising prosperity, together with religious enthusiasm, brought a massive surge in the demand for 'medieval-type' stained glass as hundreds of new churches were built in the neo-Gothic style.

The traditional craft of making windows by using separate pieces of coloured glass bound together with lead strips was revived by Thomas Willement (1786–1871) and others during the Regency period (1811–20). Within a few decades it had been embraced with passionate gusto by glass painters such as William Wailes (1808–81) and the architect Augustus Welby Northmore Pugin (1812–52), who collaborated with a Birmingham-based church decorator, John Hardman (1812–67), to reproduce authentic thirteenth-century and fourteenth-century-style glass paintings for the windows of his churches.

The middle of the nineteenth century (1850–70) saw a huge increase in the number of firms producing windows in the neo-Gothic style. Many of these studios, such as Hardman's, Clayton & Bell, Heaton, Butler & Bayne and Burlison & Grylls, worked closely with prominent ecclesiastical architects. While few windows stand out as remarkable works of art in their own right, some of the early work is impressive, with bold designs and gorgeous colours. Memorable effects could also be achieved when architects and glass painters worked together to produce unified interiors, for example the collaboration of G. F. Bodley (1827–1907) with Burlison & Grylls at Pendlebury (Manchester) and Hoar Cross (Staffordshire).

Other workshops of note included Ward & Hughes, Lavers, Barraud & Westlake, and James Powell & Sons. Some architects, such as William Burges (1827–81) and Frederick Preedy (1820–98), also designed windows.

Schemes were financed by public subscriptions and wealthy patrons to beautify new churches, often in a piecemeal way. Large numbers of windows were installed by grieving relatives as alternatives to inscribed plaques and

Opposite:
Louisa Upcher
(d. 1863, aged
fifteen), by James
Powell & Sons,
1864, All Saints,
Upper Sheringham,
Norfolk.

Window designed
by A. W. N. Pugin,
1850–2, made by
J. G. Crace, Bolton
Abbey, Yorkshire.

funerary sculpture. Some of these windows incorporated painted portraits of the deceased. At Upper Sheringham (Norfolk), an enamelled photographic image was incorporated into the window.

Styles changed from the 1870s onwards when the rigid copying of medieval designs was replaced by a more pictorial style in muted colours. There was also a preference for the late Gothic and Renaissance-influenced glass of the fifteenth and sixteenth centuries, as can be seen in the output of Charles Eamer Kempe (1837–1907) and his heir, Walter Tower. Kempe's style is easily recognisable and characterised by delicate faces and detailed costumes, often painted with large areas of silver stain, as can be seen in Burford (Oxfordshire) and West Kirby (Merseyside). Some windows include his company signature, a wheatsheaf, amended after his death by the addition of his successor's logo of a black tower.

Another prolific firm was formed by the Arts and Crafts pioneer William Morris (1834–96), who recruited artists such as Edward Burne-Jones (1833–98), Ford Madox Brown (1821–93) and Dante Gabriel Rossetti (1828–82) to design windows in the Pre-Raphaelite style of fifteenth-century Italian art. In 1875 Burne-Jones became the sole designer for the firm until his death. His windows included distinctive green and ruby red colours, naturalistic background foliage instead of mock-medieval architectural details, and softer, graceful figures in flowing drapery. Some of Burne-Jones's work was outstanding, especially the windows he made for Birmingham's Anglican Cathedral. A complete scheme of Morris & Co glass from the 1890s survives *in situ* in Manchester College, Oxford.

Over eighty thousand new windows were made between 1800 and 1900, some by workshops employing up to three hundred men – Kempe alone had around fifty staff in 1899 and supplied over 3,100 windows, including some for export. In many cases the different stages of manufacture were treated as separate industrial processes rather than as an artistic whole.

The restoration of older glass was also undertaken with often very different results. Although many important windows were saved by sensitive repair programmes, when the Shrewsbury-based firm of Betton & Evans repaired the medieval glass at Winchester College in the 1820s, they replaced the surviving fourteenth-century glass with their own copied version. Elsewhere fragments of old glass were often collected and assembled in jumbled designs.

A number of late nineteenth- and early twentieth-century windows commemorated important moments in British history, such as Queen Victoria's Diamond Jubilee in 1897 and the coronation of her son, Edward VII, in 1902. These windows served as public monuments. Others recorded the names of those who died serving her empire in the Crimea and African wars. Missionaries killed by indigenous people were also remembered, as at Broughton

Above right:
Chancel by
G. F. Bodley and
Burlison & Grylls,
1872–5, Holy
Angels, Hoar
Cross,
Staffordshire.

Above left:
St Gabriel, with
wheatsheaf
in lower left-hand
corner, by Charles
Eamer Kempe,
1901, St Mary,
Salehurst, East
Sussex.

Right: The Last
Judgement, by
Edward Burne-
Jones, installed
1897, Cathedral
of St Philip,
Birmingham, West
Midlands.

Detail from
St Michael, by
Clayton & Bell,
1860, St Mary,
Hanley Castle,
Worcestershire.

(Buckinghamshire). At Binton in Warwickshire, the church features a four-light
memorial window (1915) by Walter Tower (Kempe) depicting incidents from
Captain Robert Falcon Scott's ill-fated expedition to the South Pole in 1910–12.

Far left: Bishop
John Coleridge
Patterson (1827–
71), killed in the
Solomon Islands in
1871, St Lawrence,
Broughton,
Buckinghamshire.

Left: Captain
Oates leaves the
tent to try to save
his companions
('I am just going
outside and may
be some time'),
St Peter, Binton,
Warwickshire.

THE TWENTIETH
CENTURY TO THE
PRESENT

TOWARDS THE END of the nineteenth century a new generation of glass painters emerged who wanted to design and make their own windows, controlling every part of the process. Their work included experimentation with new techniques and a gradual abandonment of historical models. The most influential of these artist-craftsmen was Christopher Whall (1849–1924), who designed his first window in 1880, and whose work with 'slab' glass, a thick and unevenly textured product invented in 1889, can be seen in Canterbury Cathedral and the Lady Chapel of Gloucester Cathedral.

His pupils and followers included Margaret Rope (1882–1953), A.J. Davies (1877–1953), Mary Lowndes (1857–1929) and Karl Parsons (1884–1934), the most talented of the group. At Waterford (Hertfordshire), one of his windows includes layers of glass (plating) and acid etching to produce intricate effects.

Whall was also instrumental in the revival of stained glass in Ireland, which produced a series of important designers, including Harry Clarke (1889–1931), Evie Hone (1894–1955), and Wilhelmina Geddes (1887–1955).

Clarke was influenced by Art-Deco designs and used tiny pieces of glass to enrich his windows; examples can be seen at St Mary, Nantwich (Cheshire), Ashdown Park, East Grinstead (West Sussex), Sturminster Newton (Dorset), and the church of St Cuthbert, Old Elvet, Durham.

Evie Hone is best remembered for producing windows which resembled expressionist paintings in stained glass, at Wellingborough (Northamptonshire), Highgate (Greater London), and at Eton College Chapel (Berkshire), for example.

Geddes's work was passionate and sought to convey an emotional experience rather than any literal physical reality. Her figures were forceful and dramatic, her use of colours superb. Good examples of her work survive at Laleham (Surrey) and Wallsend (Tyne and Wear). Another outstanding artist was the Scottish-born Douglas Strachan (1875–1950), whose work can be seen at Thirsk (Yorkshire), Winchelsea (East Sussex) and Woldingham, (Surrey).

Opposite
Dalle de verre
windows, by Dom
Charles Norris
OSB, 1958–61,
Our Lady of
Fatima, Harlow,
Essex.

Although these artists are now much admired, for most of the inter-war years English patrons preferred designers such as Sir John Ninian Comper (1864–1960) and Christopher Webb (1886–1966) who produced

Above: A woman clothed with the sun crushing Satan (the serpent), detail from the Revelation of St John, by Christopher Whall, 1907, St John the Baptist, Burford, Oxfordshire.

Right: St Cecilia, by Karl Parsons, 1929, St Michael and All Angels, Waterford, Hertfordshire.

Opposite: The Virgin and Child with St Cecilia and Richard Coeur de Lion, by Harry Clarke, 1919, St Mary, Nantwich, Cheshire.

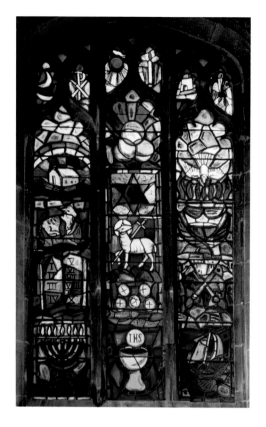

traditional figural or representational styles of painting at odds with the 'modernism' sweeping the Continent. The Anglo-Belgian artist Frank Brangwyn (1867–1956) also designed windows, as at Bucklebury (Berkshire) and Manaton (Devon). Lighter work in this period includes a five-light window by Webb's brother Geoffrey, commemorating the centenary of the birth of Charles Dodgson (Lewis Carroll, 1832–98), at Daresbury (Cheshire). Here characters from the author's best-known work, *Alice's Adventures in Wonderland*, are featured.

The years immediately after 1945 saw a huge demand for new windows to replace those blown out by enemy bombing. Considerable amounts of Victorian, and sometimes earlier, glass had been lost, including sixteenth-century angels in the west window of Henry VII's Chapel in Westminster Abbey, shattered by an air raid in 1940. Replacement windows in the Abbey chapter house include small paintings by Joan Howson (1885–1964) depicting the

Above: Symbols of the Old and New Testament, by Evie Hone, 1955, All Hallows, Wellingborough, Northamptonshire.

Right:
St Christopher,
by Wilhelmina
Geddes, 1926, All
Saints, Laleham
(Surrey).

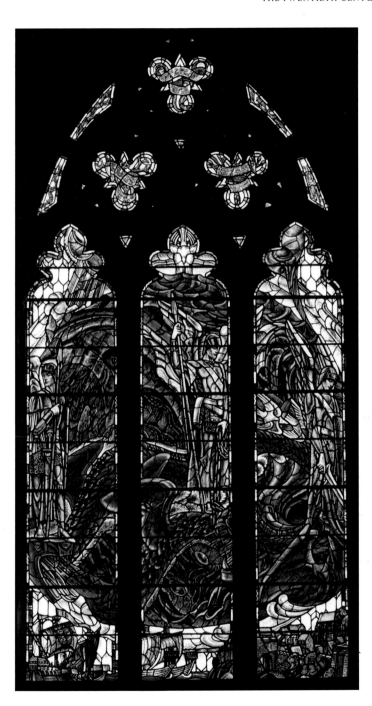

Left: 'The Sea' war
memorial window
by Douglas
Strachan, 1933,
St Thomas,
Winchelsea, East
Sussex.

Below: St Anne
teaching the Virgin
to read, by Frank
Brangwyn, 1912,
St Mary,
Bucklebury,
Berkshire.

Right: Lewis
Carroll as an
ordained deacon
with Alice, the
White Rabbit, Bill
the Lizard and the
Dodo, by Geoffrey
Webb (1879–
1954), 1935, All
Saints, Daresbury,
Cheshire.

Below: West
window, by Alfred
Wolmark, 1915,
St Mary, Slough,
Berkshire.

defence of London during the Blitz. A window in the same church by Hugh Easton (1906–65), unveiled by George VI in 1947, commemorates the fighter squadrons and pilots who served during the Battle of Britain in 1940.

Enthused by modern architecture, some artists began to design windows bursting with experimental designs, techniques, adhesives and different types of glass.

Although an abstract design had been made by Alfred Wolmark (1877–1961) for St Mary's church, Slough (Berkshire) as early as 1915, the first 'modernist' windows to make any public impact were installed in the newly built Coventry Cathedral in the 1960s. A team led by Lawrence Lee (1909–2011) made ten spectacular 70-foot-high abstract and semi-abstract windows for the nave of the church while the artists John Piper (1903–92) and Patrick Reyntiens

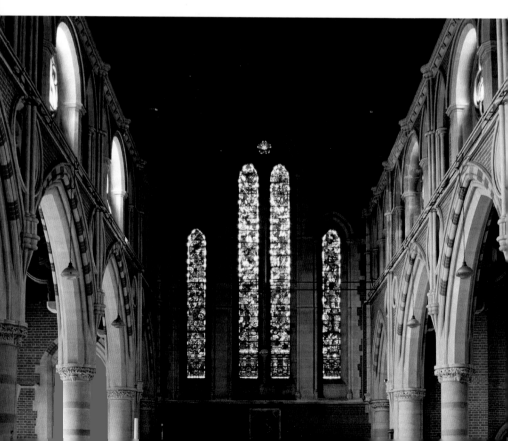

Left: Nave windows by Lawrence Lee, Geoffrey Clarke and Keith New; Baptistry window by John Piper and Patrick Reyntiens, 1962, Coventry Cathedral, West Midlands.

Below: Detail of the east window by Marc Chagall (1967), commemorating Sarah Venetia d'Avigdor-Goldsmid, who drowned in 1963, All Saints, Tudeley, Kent.

(b. 1925) glazed the baptistry in a similar style. The colours of the nave windows – green, red, multi-coloured, purple and gold – represented the progression from birth to death, with Lee's own red and gold design symbolising early manhood.

Some of the finest post-war windows were made as a result of the collaboration between Piper and Reyntiens. Another successful partnership saw windows at Chichester Cathedral and Tudeley church (Kent) designed by the Russian-Jewish artist Marc Chagall (1887–1985), and made by the French glass painter Charles Marcq (1923–2006).

Four other important post-war artists were Ervin Bossanyi (1891–1975), Margaret Traherne (1919–2006), John Hayward (1929–2007) and Alan Younger (1933–2004). Bossanyi was a Hungarian refugee, whose designs were strongly influenced by central European folk art. The themes of his

Detail from the 'Salvation' window, by Ervin Bossanyi, 1958, Canterbury Cathedral, Kent.

'Peace' and 'Salvation' windows at Canterbury Cathedral were particularly relevant to survivors of the Second World War. The 18-foot-high 'Peace' window shows Christ freeing a captive from a prison which has a swastika design on the keyhole of its padlock.

Traherne admired French expressionist painters and also produced abstract windows in coloured *dalle de verre*, a type of thick slab glass

usually cast in 1-inch thicknesses and set in a concrete or resin matrix. Good examples of her work can be seen at Wootton Wawen (Warwickshire), and the Lady Chapel in Liverpool's Roman Catholic Cathedral. Tiles of *dalle de verre* in brilliant colours were used by Dom Charles Norris OSB (1901–2004) at Buckfast Abbey (Devon) and at Harlow (Essex).

A fine example of Hayward's work can be seen at the church of St Mary-le-Bow in the City of London, while Younger made a notable rose window for St Albans Cathedral (Hertfordshire).

In 1980 Salisbury Cathedral installed an intensely dark blue 'Prisoner of Conscience' window by the French artist Gabriel Loire (1904–96).

St Kenelm, by Margaret Traherne, 1958, St Peter, Wootton Wawen, Warwickshire.

'Prisoner of Conscience', by Gabriel Loire, 1980, Salisbury Cathedral, Wiltshire.

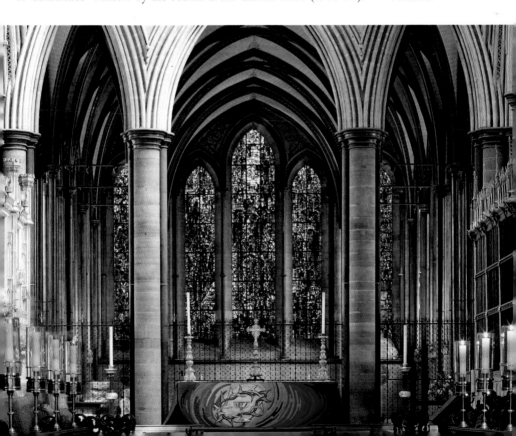

Conservators at Barley Studios in York examining sixteenth-century glass from the Lady Chapel, Lichfield Cathedral, Staffordshire.

Revelation window, by Tony Hollaway, 1995, Manchester Cathedral.

Five windows for the west end of Manchester Cathedral made by Tony Hollaway (1928–2000) between 1973 and 1995 have been described as having an 'ineffable spiritual quality'.

Irrespective of the styles or fashions that have appeared over the past fifteen hundred years, stained glass remains a uniquely demanding art. Apart from requiring excellent drawing skills and the ability to create original designs which harmonise paint and meaning, artists need to master form and line, and the role of cut lines and leading in compositions, fully understand the texture, depth, colour, and light values of glass, and be able to visualise how their glass will complement buildings and be seen, at dawn and dusk, in summer sunshine and through the gloom of a wintry day. Fortunately a number of talented artists continue the tradition today.

At the same time the conservation of this important heritage is proving ever more urgent. English churches are custodians of huge galleries of painted and stained glass, which deserves the same care as other major works of art. Congregations, skilled conservators, specialist art historians, and charitable organisations are working together to save this precious legacy.

It is a challenge that must not fail.

FURTHER READING

Brown, Sarah, and O'Connor, David. *Medieval Craftsmen: Glass-Painters*, British Museum Press, 1991.

Brown, Sarah, and MacDonald, L. *Fairford Parish Church: A Medieval Church and its Stained Glass*. Sutton Publishing, 2007.

Cannon, Linda. *Stained Glass in the Burrell Collection*. W. & R. Chambers, 1991.

Cowen, Painton. *The Rose Window*. Thames & Hudson, 2005.

Cowen, Painton. *English Stained Glass*. Thames & Hudson, 2008.

Harrison, Martin. *Victorian Stained Glass*. Barrie & Jenkins, 1980.

Journal of Stained Glass. Published annually by the British Society of Master Glass Painters. Includes articles about new commissions.

Lee, Lawrence. *The Appreciation of Stained Glass*. Oxford University Press, 1977.

Lee, Lawrence; Seddon, George; and Stephens, Francis. *Stained Glass*. Mitchell Beazley, 1976.

Marks, Richard. *Stained Glass in England during the Middle Ages*. Routledge, 1993.

Piper, John. *Stained Glass: Art or Anti-Art*. Studio Vista, 1968.

Raguin, Virginia Chieffo. *The History of Stained Glass*. Thames & Hudson, 2003.

Reyntiens, Patrick. *The Technique of Stained Glass*. Batsford, 1977.

Williamson, P. *Medieval and Renaissance Stained Glass in the Victoria and Albert Museum*. V&A Publications, 2003.

See also: volumes published by the GB Committee of the Corpus Vitrearum Medii Aevi (CVMA), an international research project dedicated to recording medieval stained glass. The website includes twenty thousand images of stained glass in England: www.cvma.ac.uk

WEBSITES

Vidimus: free online magazine on medieval stained glass published by the GB Committee of the CVMA. www.vidimus.org

The Rose Window: website with over 17,000 images of English and French stained glass. www.therosewindow.com

KEY ORGANISATIONS

Association for the History of Glass
www.historyofglass.org.uk/
The British Society of Master Glass Painters
www.bsmgp.org.uk

Corpus Vitrearum Medii Aevi
www.cvma.ac.uk
Institute of Conservation
www.icon.org.uk
Worshipful Company of Glaziers and Painters of Glass
www.worshipfulglaziers.com

PLACES TO VISIT

This Gazetteer lists nearly 600 places where important stained glass can be seen. It is advisable to check accessibility in advance of a visit. The numbers in the list refer to centuries. Entries with * denote foreign glass.

Bedfordshire: Cockayne Hatley 14, 15, 18. Luton: St Mary 15, 19, 20. Northill 17, 19. Totternhoe 20.

Berkshire: Aldermaston 13. Bracknell: St Michael & St Mary 19. Bucklebury 17, 20. Cookham Dean 19. Eton College Chapel 20. Pangbourne 19, 20. Slough: St Mary 19, 20. Warfield 14, 19, 20. Wasing 16, 17*, 19, 20, 21. Windsor: St George's Chapel 16, 20.

Bristol: Bristol: All Saints, Clifton 20; All Saints, Corn Street, 20; Bristol Cathedral 14, 15, 19, 20; St Mark, College Green (Lord Mayor's Chapel) 16, 17*; St Mary Redcliffe 15, 19, 20.

Buckinghamshire: Addington 16, 17 *. Bradenham 16, 18, 19. Chetwode 13, 14. Drayton Beauchamp 15. Frieth 19. Hillesden 16. Marlow 19. Stoke Poges 16, 17, 19, 20. Turville 16, 18, 20.

Cambridgeshire: Cambridge: All Saints Jesus Lane, 19, 20; Christ's College 15, 16, 19; Corpus Christi College 16, 19*; Jesus College 19; King's College 16; Peterhouse 17, 19; Robinson College 20; St John's College 19; Trinity College 18, 19; Westminster College 20. Doddington 19. Ely Cathedral 14, 19, 20 and Stained Glass Museum (all periods). Kimbolton 15, 20. Leverington 15. Meldreth 14, 19. Peterborough Cathedral 19. St Neots 19. Thorney 15, 19. Wisbech St Mary 15*, 19. Wistow 15.

Cheshire: Acton 19. Astbury 15. Birtles 16, 17*. Chester Cathedral 19. Daresbury 20. Disley 16. Grappenhall 14, 19. Malpas 16*. Nantwich 14, 19, 20. Neston 19. Warrington 19. Wilmslow 20.

Cornwall: Cotehele, Cotehele House (NT) 16. Ladock 19. Lostwithiel 19. St Kew 15. St Neot 15, 16. St Winnow 15, 16. Truro Cathedral 19.

Cumbria: Ambleside 19. Bowness-on-Windermere 15. Brampton 19. Carlisle Cathedral 14, 19. Cartmel Fell 14, 15. Cartmel Priory 14, 15,

19. Casterton 19. Greystoke 15. Kirkampton 19. Kirkby-in-Furness
12. Lanercost Priory 19, 20. Troutbeck 19.

Derbyshire: Ashbourne 13, 14, 15, 19, 20. Chesterfield: St Mary 19, 20.
Dalbury 12. Darley Dale 19. Derby Cathedral 20. Morley 15. Norbury
14, 15. Staveley 14, 17, 20. Tideswell 19. Wilne 17.

Devon: Ashton 15. Bampton 15. Bere Ferrers 14. Buckfast Abbey 20.
Clovelly 19, 20. Doddiscombsleigh 15, 19, 20. Exeter Cathedral 14,
15, 16, 18, 19, 20. Ilfracombe 19. Ottery St Mary 19. Plymouth: St
Andrew 20. Tavistock 19. Tiverton 19. Torquay: St John 19.

Dorset: Abbotsbury 15, 18. Bournemouth: St Peter 19; St Stephen 19.
Bradford Peverell 15, 19. Cattistock 19, 20. Melbury Bubb 15. Milton
Abbas: Milton Abbey 15, 19. Sherborne: Almshouse of St John 15;
Sherborne Abbey 15, 19, 20. Sturminster Newton 19, 20. Trent 16, 17,
19*. Wimborne Minster 16, 19.

Durham: Darlington: St Cuthbert 19. Durham: Cathedral 14, 15, 19, 20,
21; St Cuthbert 20; St Oswald 19. Lanchester 13*. Raby Castle 12, 13,
16*.

Essex: Audley End (English Heritage) 18. Basildon: St Martin 20.
Chelmsford Cathedral 19, 20. Clavering 15. Harlow: Our Lady of
Fatima 20; St Mary (Old Harlow) 14, 18, 19. Heybridge 13, 20. Little
Easton 17. Margaretting 15. Messing 17. Prittlewell 16*. Rivenhall 12,
13*. Saffron Walden 19. Thaxted 14, 15. Waltham Abbey 19, 20.

Gloucestershire: Arlingham 14, 15. Bagendon 15, 19, 20. Bibury 13,
19, 20. Bromsberrow 17, 19. Buckland 15. Cheltenham: St
Christopher (Warden Hill) 20; St Mary 19. Cirencester 15. Deerhurst
14. Fairford 16. Gloucester Cathedral 14, 15, 19, 20. North Cerney
15, 20. Prinknash Abbey 20. Selsley 19. Temple Guiting 15. Tewkesbury
Abbey 14, 19.

Hampshire: Basingstoke: All Saints 19, 20; St Michael 16, 17, 20.
Bramley 14, 16*. East Tytherley 13, 14. Fareham 18. Grateley 13.
Lyndhurst: St Michael & All Angels 19. Rownhams 16 *. Selborne 20.
The Vyne (NT) 16, 18. Winchester: Cathedral 15, 16, 19, 20; St Cross
Hospital 15, 19; Winchester College 14, 15, 19.

Herefordshire: Abbey Dore 15, 16, 17. Brinsop 14, 20. Brockhampton-
by-Ross 20. Credenhill 14. Eaton Bishop 14. Hereford Cathedral 14,
19, 20, 21. Ledbury 13, 16, 19, 20. Madley 13, 14. Ross-on-Wye: St
Mary 15. Sellack 15, 16, 17.

Hertfordshire: Aldbury 16*. Aldenham 19. Barkway 14, 15.
Berkhamsted 19. Bishop's Stortford 19. Bourne End 19. Chipping
Barnet 19. Furneux Pelham 19. Hatfield House Chapel 17. King's
Walden 19. St Albans Cathedral 19, 20. St Paul's Walden 14, 20. Ware
19, 20. Waterford 19, 20.

Isle of Wight: Bonchurch 19. Newport 19. Ventnor 19.

Kent: Bishopsbourne 13, 16. Brabourne 12, 15. Canterbury Cathedral 12, 13, 15, 20. Chartham 14. Chevening 20. Cobham 19, 20. Cranbrook 16. Edenbridge 19. Hastingleigh 13. Lamberhurst 20. Lullingstone 14, 16, 18. Maidstone: All Saints 19; St Michael & All Angels 19. Marden 20. Mereworth 16, 17, 18. Mersham 15. Nackington 13. Nettlestead 15. Patrixbourne 17 *. Penshurst 19, 20. Ramsgate: St Augustine 19. Rochester Cathedral 19. Selling 14. Sevenoaks: St Nicholas 19. Tudeley 20. Westwell 13, 14.

Lancashire: Blackburn: Cathedral 19, 20; St Gabriel 20. Burnley: All Saints, Habergham 20. Leyland: St Mary (RC) 20. Longridge 20. Lytham St Annes 19. Tunstall 15, 16, 20.

Leicestershire: Appleby Magna 14. Ashby-de-la-Zouch 16*. Hallaton 19. Leicester: Cathedral 20; Museum 15, 16. Loughborough 19, 20. Stockerston 15. Thornton 14. Twycross 12, 13*. Withcote 16.

Lincolnshire: Barton-upon-Humber 14, 19, 20. Boston: St Botolph 19, 20. Gedney 14. Grantham 19, 20. Heydour 14, 15. Lincoln: All Saints 20; Lincoln Cathedral 12, 13, 14, 18, 19, 20. Raithby-by-Louth 19. Redbourne 19. Ruskington 19. Stamford: Browne's Hospital 15; St George 15, 18; St Martin 15, 16, 19; St Mary 19. Tattershall 15. Wrangle 14.

Greater London: Battersea: St Mary 17, 20. Bromley: St Mary 20. Chelsea: Holy Trinity 19, 20; St Simon Zelotes 21. Chipping Barnet 19. Downe 20. Hampton Court Palace 19. Highgate: St Michael 20. Holborn: Lincoln's Inn Chapel 17; Sir John Soane Museum 16, 17, 18. Kensington: Victoria and Albert Museum (all periods). Orpington: Holy Innocents 20. Southwark: Cathedral 19, 20. Twickenham: Strawberry Hill 16, 17, 20. Walthamstow: William Morris Gallery 19, 20. Westminster: All Saints, Margaret Street 15, 19; Savoy Chapel 20; St George, Hanover Square, 16*; St Margaret, Parliament Square 16; Westminster Abbey 13, 15, 18, 19, 20. Wimbledon: St Mary 14, 17, 20.

City of London: St Andrew Undershaft 17; St Botolph, Aldersgate 18, 19, 20; St Ethelburga, Bishopsgate 21; St Mary-le-Bow 20; St Stephen Walbrook 20; Temple church 20.

Greater Manchester (includes former parts of Lancashire and Cheshire): Ashton-under-Lyne 15. Manchester: Manchester Cathedral 20; St Chrysostom 19, 20. Marple 19, 20. Middleton 16, 20. Pendlebury 19.

Merseyside (includes former parts of Lancashire and Cheshire): Allerton: All Hallows 19. Liverpool: Anglican Cathedral 20; RC Cathedral: 20. Port Sunlight 20. St Helens: Pilkington Glass Museum (all periods). West Kirby 19.

Norfolk: Bale 14, 15. Chedgrave 16, 17*. East Harling 15. Elsing 14. Harpley 15. Hevingham 16*. Hingham 16*. Kimberley 14, 16. Martham 15, 19. Mileham 14, 15. Mulbarton 16, 19. North Tuddenham 15. Norwich: Cathedral 16, 19, 20; Guildhall 15; St Peter Hungate 15, 16; St Peter Mancroft 15, 20; St Stephen 16. Ringland 15. Salle 15. Saxlingham Nethergate 13, 14, 15, 19, 20. Scole 20. Sculthorpe 19. Stody 15. Stradsett 16*. Thursford 19. Thurton 15, 16*,19. Warham 15, 16*.

Northamptonshire: Abington 20. Aldwincle: St Peter 14, 21. Apethorpe 17, 18. Great Weldon 14, 16, 20. Lowick 14. Middleton Cheney 19. Rushden 15. Stanford-on-Avon 14, 15, 16, 19. Wellingborough: All Hallows 20; St Mary 20.

Northumberland: Alnwick 15, 19. Berwick-upon-Tweed 16*. Morpeth 14.

Nottinghamshire: Bleasby 20. Fledborough 12, 14. Holme-by-Newark 12, 15, 16. Hucknall Torkard 19. Misterton 20. Newark 14, 15, 19. Nottingham: St Barnabas (RC Cathedral) 19, 20; St Mary 15, 19. Southwell Minster 14, 16, 17, 19, 20. Strelley 14, 16, 17, 19.

Oxfordshire: Beckley 14. Bledington 15. Bloxham 19. Burford 15, 19, 20. Cassington 14, 15, 16*. Childrey 15. Chinnor 14, 19, 20. Dorchester Abbey 13, 14, 19. Iffley 15, 20. Kidlington 13, 15, 19. Nettlebed 20. North Moreton 14. Oxford: All Souls College 15, 19; Balliol College 16, 17, 19; Brasenose College 18, 19; Christ Church Cathedral 14, 17, 19; Corpus Christi College 20; Exeter College 19; Jesus College 19; Keble College 19; Lincoln College 17; Magdalen College 17; Mansfield College 19; Merton College 14, 15, 18; New College 14, 18, 21; Nuffield College 20; Oriel College 16, 15, 18, 19; Queen's College 16, 17, 18; St Edmund Hall 19; St John's College 19, 20; St Peter's College 20; Trinity College 14, 15, 16, 17, 19; University College 17, 19; Wadham College 17; Worcester College 19; St Mary (University Church) 19; St Michael at the North Gate 13, 15. Radley 16. Shiplake 15*. Stanton St John 13, 14. Waterperry 14, 15, 16. Yarnton 15, 16, 17.

Rutland: Ayston 15. Clipsham 15. North Luffenham 14, 19.

Shropshire: Bromfield 16, 19. Ludlow: St Laurence 14, 15, 19, 20. Meole Brace 19. Shrewsbury: St Alkmund 18; St Chad 19; St Julian 16*; St Mary 14, 15, 16, 17, 19*. Upton Magna 19.

Somerset: Bath: Bath Abbey 17, 19, 20; St Bartholomew 20. East Brent 15. Farleigh Hungerford 15, 16. Glastonbury: St John the Baptist, 15, 19, 20. Langport 15, 19. Low Ham 17. Orchardleigh 15. Trull 15. Wells Cathedral 14, 15, 17, 18, 19, 20. Winscombe 15, 16, 19.

Staffordshire: Amington 19. Checkley 14. Cheddleton 19. Enville 14, 19, 21. Hamstall Ridware 14, 16, 19. Hoar Cross 19. Lichfield Cathedral

16*, 19. Rolleston 14, 15. Tamworth 19, 20. Wombourne 19.

Suffolk: Aldeburgh 20. Bardwell 15. Blaxhall 20. Blythburgh 15. Brandon 19, 20. Bury St Edmunds: Cathedral 16*, 19; St Mary 19. Combs 15. Depden 14, 16. Elveden 19, 20. Great Saxham 16*. Herringfleet 14, 15, 16*, 19. Herringswell 20. Icklingham 14. Ipswich: St Mary le Tower 19; St Matthew 19. Long Melford 15. Lowestoft: St Margaret 19, 20. Norton 15. Nowton 16, 17*. Snape 20.

Surrey: Abinger 20. Ashtead 16*. Compton 13, 16*. Gatton 16, 17*. Great Bookham 15*. Guildford: Abbot's Hospital 17; Cathedral 20. Haslemere 17, 19. Laleham 20. Ockham 15, 18, 19, 20. Peper Harow 19. Stoke d'Abernon 15, 16, 17*. Thursley 15 *. Titsey 19. West Horsley 13, 20. Woldingham 20.

Sussex, East and West: Arundel: St Philip Neri, 19. Bexhill: St Peter 15. Brighton: St Michael & All Angels 19; St Paul 19. Chichester: Cathedral 19, 20; St Richard 20. Cuckfield 19. Eastbourne: St Mary 20. Horsham: St Mary 19. Lodsworth 19, 20. Pagham 16*, 19. Rotherfield 19. Rottingdean 19. Salehurst 15. Ticehurst 15, 19. Winchelsea 15, 20. Woolbeding 16*.

Tyne and Wear: Jarrow: St Paul; Bede's World Museum 8. Newcastle-upon-Tyne: Cathedral 15, 19, 20; St Andrew 19, 20; St John the Baptist 20. Sunderland: Christchurch 19. Wallsend, St Luke 20.

Warwickshire: Binton 20. Chadshunt 16*. Charlecote 19. Cherington 14, 15, 16. Coughton 16. Ettington Park 20. Fillongley 14, 15, 16. Hampton Lucy 19. Mancetter 14. Merevale 14, 15. Warwick: St Mary 15, 19, 20. Weston-on-Avon 15. Willoughby 20. Wootton Wawen 15, 20.

West Midlands: Binley 18. Birmingham: Anglican Cathedral (St Philip) 19; RC Cathedral (St Chad) 19. Cheylesmore 20. Coventry: Cathedral 15, 20; St Mary's Hall 15, 20. Wolverhampton: St Andrew 20.

Wiltshire: Chippenham: St Andrew 20. Clyffe Pypard 16, 17*. Crudwell 15. Edington 15. Laverstock 13, 19. Lydiard Tregoze (house and church) 15, 17. Marlborough 19. Mere 14, 19. Oaksey 15. Rodbourne 19. Salisbury: Cathedral 13, 14, 17, 18, 19, 20; St Thomas 15. Teffont Evias 16, 17*. Wilton 12, 13, 14, 15, 16, 17*.

Worcestershire: Bredon 14, 19, 20. Bromsgrove 19. Bushley 19, 20. Chaddesley Corbett 19, 20. Crowle 15, 19. Evesham: All Saints 19, 20; St Lawrence 19, 20. Fladbury 14, 19. Great Malvern Priory 15, 19, 21. Great Witley 18. Hanbury 19. Hanley Castle 19. Himbleton 13, 15, 19, 20. Kemerton 19. Kempsey 14. Little Malvern 15. Mamble 14. Martley 20. Oddingley 16. Pershore Abbey 19. Upton-on-Severn 19, 20. Warndon 14, 15. Whittington 19. Wilden 20. Worcester Cathedral 19.

Yorkshire, East: Beverley Minster 13, 14, 15, 19, 21. Ellerton 21. Harpham 18. Hotham 20. South Dalton 19.

Yorkshire, North: Acaster Malbis 14. Baldersby 19. Bolton Abbey 19. Bolton Percy 15. Coxwold 15, 18. Denton-in-Wharfedale 17. Knaresborough 19. Ripon Cathedral 15, 19. Scarborough 19. Selby Abbey 14, 19. Tadcaster 14, 15, 19, 20. York: All Saints, North Street 14, 15; All Saints, Pavement 14; Holy Trinity, Goodramgate 15; St Denys, Walmgate 14, 15; St Helen, Stonegate 14, 15, 16; St Martin-cum-Gregory 15; St Martin-le-Belfry 14; St Martin-le-Grand 15; St Michael, Spurriergate 15, 16; York Minster 13, 14, 15, 16, 17, 18, 19, 20; Yorkshire Museum (all periods).

Yorkshire, South: Doncaster: St George 19. Rotherham 19. Sheffield Cathedral 19, 20.

Yorkshire, West: Adel 18. Almondbury 15. Bingley 19. Bradford Cathedral 19, 20. Elland 15, 19. Ilkley 19, 20. Leeds: St John the Baptist 18; St Peter 19. Methley 15, 19, 20. Thornhill 15, 18. Wragby 16. 17, 18*.

Tracery light,
fifteenth century,
St Leonard,
Bledington,
Oxfordshire.

INDEX

Page numbers in italics refer to illustrations